MAREEN OLIVER

STAINED by HIS BLOOD

FOR HIS PURPOSE

To My friend Shujuan & My Brother Shujuan May God Bless You in all you do. Love always, Mareen Oliver 10-13

This book is a teaching and learning tool therefore, some phrases and words are repeated continuously throughout this book on purpose.

STAINED by HIS BLOOD

STAINED by HIS BLOOD

FOR HIS PURPOSE

Copyright © 2005 Mareen Oliver

All Scripture quotations, unless otherwise indicated, are taken from the Authorized King James Version.

All rights reserved. No part of this book may be used or reproduced by any means, graphic, electronic, or mechanical, including photocopying, recording, taping or by any information storage retrieval system without the written permission of the publisher.
The use of short quotations or occasional page copying for personal or group study is, permitted and encouraged.

For speaking engagements, contact:
Minister Mareen Oliver
Sleeping With The Word Outreach Ministries
P.O. Box 3205 Oak Park IL, 60303
or
Email: stainedbyhisblood1@gmail.com

DEDICATION

To my awesome husband and best friend Robert G. Oliver Sr. Thank you for being there and loving me as you love yourself. I thank our Heavenly Father for you every day. God gave me his best; you are such a man of God! Love you always.

To our four wonderful children, He has blessed us with, Robert (RJ), Ebonee, Brandy and Tanisha may you continue to allow God to use you for His glory! Our prayers are always with you. We Love You.

Ms. Daisy M. Peoples, you are my mother and friend, I have learned so much from you, you are such a woman of God! I Praise and thank Him for you.

Ms. Everett R. Oliver, you are a sweet and kind mother in law and I am so glad, God has blessed me with you in my life.

Lee A. Peoples, my dad without you there would not have been me. Momma Katherine Peoples what a beautiful stepmom you are, I love you and dad very much.

STAINED by HIS BLOOD

ACKNOWLEGEMENTS

My Heavenly Father, All Glory and Honor unto you. Thank you for anointing me to write, to share with others your love. Thank you for letting the truth be known, that you came that we might have life, and that we might have it more abundantly.

Thanks to my Pastor Dr. Bill Winston for teaching the Word of God with simplicity and boldness so that I could complete what our Father God has put before me to write, "Whether you receive the manifestation of your healing or not does not change the truth that God is still a Healer".

Pastor Barnett, thank you, for being a man of God, one who walks in integrity.

You know when you are going through something that seems so much bigger than you are and you ask God for help, He sends you what you need the most. I thank God for the prayers and encouragement from these special people while the Holy Spirit helped me stay in faith for my victory:

Thank you, **Mary Carrell**, *my bible class teacher for letting the Holy Ghost lead you in your teachings.*
Loretta Allen, *thank you for the book and for those prophetic words.*
Thank you, **Christ Tabernacle Combined Choir**, *under the leadership of the late Rev. Milton Brunson.*

Special Shout Out To:
Jewel Brewer, thank you for your support and encouragement on all I set out to do, love you girl.

Mary Square, my goddaughter you are such a unique woman of God, thank you for your input and encouragement.

Naomi Malcolm, thank you for believing in me and giving me your creative mind and sense of humor.

STAINED by HIS BLOOD

Note: If you are taking medication or treatments for whatever it is that you have being diagnosed with, you should continue to take it as instructed, unless you have been told by your physician, or The Holy Spirit, otherwise continue to take your medicine as usual, and do not feel guilty. The author is not a physician. She is just sharing her testimony and The Word of God with you.

STAINED by HIS BLOOD

CONTENTS

	INTRODUCTION	8
1	THE ENDING	18
2	HUMBLE BEGINNINGS	33
3	TRANSITION AND RESTORATION	43
4	DESIRES	52
5	TWO BECOMING ONE	62
6	MY NAME IS EBONEE	78
7	SECOND OPINION PLEASE	96
8	DO NOT RECEIVE THAT!	104
9	I HAVE THE VICTORY	116
10	WHOSE REPORT WILL YOU BELIEVE?	126
11	SPEAK THE WORD ONLY	143
12	PERSECUTION, PRAYER AND PRAISE	158
13	ALL IS WELL	173
14	MANIFESTATION	188
15	THE BEGINNING	201
16	7 STEPS WHILE WAITING FOR HEALING	211
	PRAYER OF SALVATION	244
	PRAYER FOR BAPTISM OF THE HOLY SPIRIT	247

STAINED by HIS BLOOD

STAINED by HIS BLOOD

INTRODUCTION

We as the body of Christ face many situations and circumstances just as the world does. The choices we have are to stand in faith or run in fear. When we use God's word in faith, the enemy flees. We can overcome the spirit of fear by praying, praising, worshipping and spending time in The Word and with God. This helps our faith to grow stronger, and discourages us from walking in fear. I sometimes sing praises unto God in my spiritual language (tongues) and the spirit of fear leaves.

When we use these weapons, the devil will run because he remembers what Jesus did to him when he died on Cavalry and what is going to happen to him in the end. We must decide to walk in faith and stand or walk in fear and run.

STAINED by HIS BLOOD

Let us talk about walking in faith or running in fear. When given an evil report from the doctor this report may be a shock to us upon our first time hearing it and its ok, but what matters is what we do and say next.

Our father teaches us to *walk by faith* and *that it is impossible to please him without it*. When an evil report about our health is given, I am sure we do not think about the Kingdom of God and how there is still work to be done, or souls to be saved. When given an evil report who thinks about these things, most of us do not.

Maybe, we think on how to get better and I say the word *maybe*, because some of us just receive whatever is given to us. We receive it as the final word and just die. Although it is up to the individual to either fight it, or just go home wherever that might be, heaven or hell.

STAINED by HIS BLOOD

If we choose to go home, those of us who are in Christ Jesus, I am sure our heavenly father God would welcome us. However, *LISTEN!* We do not have to go home because we have been diagnosed with an illness or disease.

Just do not claim it to be yours (my arthritis, my high blood pressure, my cancer etc.). Jesus took it all to the cross over two thousand years ago when he destroyed the enemy's power over sickness and diseases. He defeated the father of it all, the devil. I do not believe that it is a sin to have the symptoms of a cold or having been, diagnosed with a sickness or disease. I believe it is a sin if you receive it and take it to be yours. We have just denied our father God **that gave his only begotten son and our brother Jesus Christ (John 3:16)** who took all sicknesses and diseases with Him to the cross over two thousand years ago.

STAINED by HIS BLOOD

How Dare We Look At It As If It Never Happened! Let us not decide to go home to our heavenly Father because we do not want to fight a good fight of faith. Seek His Word! He did not raise us that way, if I may say it this way; I mean to run because the enemy says, Boo! With the diagnoses of sickness and disease. Say, Boo! Back, with The Word "By Jesus Stripes, I am Healed".

We are not cowards, we are not fatherless we have a Father that is bigger and larger than any father there is or ever will be. Why are we so afraid and scared of the things that the devil throws at us? Sometimes we have to go back and read, and meditate The Word of God. We need to follow, mimic, and copy the life of Jesus. We are to be just like Him. I did not read anywhere, where it says, Jesus ran from the devil. He knew who He was and who His Father is.

You have the Power of God in you through Jesus Christ. You have the same anointing power for your healing to manifest if you faint not.

STAINED by HIS BLOOD

The battle was fought and won already. Jesus won the battle over two thousand years ago. I know I have said this numerous of times, but we have to get this! All we have to do is have faith in Him and obey His Word. I know we are still stuck at it is about me! Yes, it is about you but it does not stop there, it is about our faith in God and Him using us to draw all men unto Him through our lives and testimonies.

The devil sees something great in you; he knows that you are not just a hearer of the Word but a doer *at least some of us are.* You have something that will make a difference in the Kingdom of God and destroy the devil's kingdom, therefore sickness and disease is two of the ways he wants to destroy you.

Your faith will be what God will use to fulfill His will in your life and in The Kingdom of God. The enemy figures if he can kill you with sickness and disease or the cares of this world then, the purpose that God has for your life will not be fulfilled.

STAINED by HIS BLOOD

Most of us will stay here and fight the good fight of faith and fulfill the purpose that we were born and chosen to fulfill in the body of Christ. We have the power to fulfill and complete the Will of God. Our Heavenly Father has already given us everything we need to get the job done, because guess what? He knew that the devil would come, to try to distract us or try some of his tricks to deceive us, just as he tried to do to Jesus when he was led into the wilderness in Matthew 4:1. The Holy Spirit was with Jesus, and The Holy Spirit will be with you if you want Him to be. Do not be afraid, Welcome Him in!

He will guide you and bring all things (The Word) to your remembrance. He will comfort you, as you need Him. **We have a right to be healed!**

Remember God did not put this sickness on anyone. This is not a way that He shows us his love.

STAINED by HIS BLOOD

He does not have sickness and disease in Him; therefore, He cannot give what He does not have. The devil has all the diseases and he does not mind giving it freely for your life, if you do not mind receiving it freely for his life, which is death.

The devil comes to kill, steal and destroy us of our time and our life. Jesus came that we might have life, and that we might have it more abundantly says, John 10:10.

Why not allow God to use us to show someone that he still heals or He is a surgeon in the operating room. He never changes; His word is true if you stand on it and it is true if you do not stand on it.

Know this, everything God has said to you. He will bring it to pass. One of the things I love about our Father God is, He does not lie to us. He told us this in Numbers 23:19, **God is not a man that he should lie; neither the son of man, that he should repent: hath he said, and shall he not do it? Or hath he spoken, and shall he not make it good?** Delight yourself in His word, Overdose on it, take your healing by faith, and watch it happen.

Someone will hear about it and want to know Him as their Healer, and will be encouraged to fulfill their calling in the kingdom of God.

Someone would want what God has for them, His life for theirs, all because we decided to use our faith and not fear.

CHAPTER 1

The Ending

STAINED by HIS BLOOD

I was born and raised in Chicago, Illinois and I am the oldest of four children born to Lee and Daisy Peoples—my siblings are Marsha, Sheree and Michael. Our parents separated when I was seven or eight years old. After their separation, I do not remember doing many things that children did such as, riding a bike or jumping rope....

Marsha and I took care of the two younger siblings, though we were children ourselves. We would comb their hair, hem their clothes, cook and wash dishes. Marsha and I would also wash clothes to help our mom. At that time, we had an old- fashioned washer with a wringer on it. I remember momma saying, "Y'all be careful, don't get your hands or fingers caught in the wringer!"

I would go to the corner store by myself and most of the time, I would remember what to buy but other times I had to have a list.

STAINED by HIS BLOOD

I did all of these things at an early age and yet I still did not know how to do something as simple as, tying my shoe strings or shoe laces.

Our neighborhood consisted of a lot of children and everyone, knew your business.

We could stay out late only if our parents were out with us. We would play games such as, hide-n-seek and red light- green light.

We lived in the basement of a two-story apartment building. We had to go out of a door, by the furnace, in order to get to the bathroom. I did not like it because it was scary and cold.

STAINED by HIS BLOOD

I remember momma and daddy trying to take me out there to show me that there was no reason to be afraid. I remember kicking and screaming, *"No! I don't want to go out there!"* Momma had this braided rug with fringes on each end of the rug that met you at the door once you opened it, well let's just say children have a tendency to see things differently from adults—I thought the braids were worms coming out of the rug (*satan's trick*).

Later after momma and daddy separated, Momma had to take a job working the third shift because that was all she could find. One night while my sisters were sleeping, I had to go to the bathroom. I opened the door and I began to walk—thank God, momma had removed that rug. However, near the bathroom, I heard a sound, I looked up, and there was a black cat walking across the clothesline looking down at me, with green eyes as he was meowing.

STAINED by HIS BLOOD

I ran back into the house, quickly, closed, and locked the door, and decided I was going to hold it until morning! I woke up the next morning and heard momma singing she had come in from her night job. She was washing and hanging clothes on the same clothesline where I had seen that black cat walking. I "attempted" to get up, and standing along the bed, GLARING AT ME was that same black cat. I guess momma had found herself a pet—*as if the four of us were not enough to take care of.*

When momma worked nights, most of the time she had one of her friends come over to watch us during the night and to see us off to school the following morning. After a while, momma's friend moved away. My grandmother, Sadie Bland, affectionately called "Big Momma", and my two aunts, uncle and two cousins Maria and Elaine all lived next door.

STAINED by HIS BLOOD

We went to their house if we needed something. Big Momma would come by and check on us occasionally during the evenings. The nights that we were alone, Marsha and I would take care of the younger siblings. Sometimes they would give us a hard time by not wanting to listen to us. I remember one time Michael wanted to have his way when I told him to sit down so that I could keep an eye on him. I hit him on his behind and he hollered so loud you would have thought that I really hurt him. He calmed down, fell asleep, and woke up, just as mom was coming in the door the following morning. He started back crying trying to get me in trouble, it didn't work. One night after mom left for work, we stayed up, watched TV, and cooked French fries. We used the bottom of the oven to cook and then we would fall asleep after we got finished eating. We always remembered to turn the oven off.

STAINED by HIS BLOOD

In the mornings, Marsha and I would, get Sheree washed up, and ready for school before it was time for us to walk to school.

Sheree rode a school bus for the physically challenged. We had to pick her up to put her on the bus because she couldn't walk...she crawled, having been diagnosed with cerebral palsy from birth, it wasn't easy but she never let the cerebral palsy stop her from getting around.

One day I came home from school; I noticed momma was asleep in the living room on the couch, which was located beneath two windows that sat ground level because we lived in a basement apartment. Sitting on that very window ledge was a big rat! I guess he thought he would pay us a visit....

The rat looked at me with its beady eyes and I hollered "MOM!"—while pointing at the rat.

STAINED by HIS BLOOD

Momma opened her eyes and looked, she then jumped up; she grabbed a broom that was nearby and chased it.

About this time, I was up on top of the other couch still pointing in the direction of where the rat was going. *"There it is, there it is", I yelled.*

Momma chased the rat out to the front door and into a drainage hole (where the water went when it rained). It never had a cover on it. She then grabbed a pot of hot boiling water off the stove that she kept there to keep the kitchen warm; and poured it down the hole where the rat ran into. We heard that rat scream like a squeaking cat. If momma was afraid she did not show it. I use to think that parents were not afraid of anything. That was not the first or the last time that rats and mice visited or moved in our house, *where was God? I thought.*

STAINED by HIS BLOOD

One night, momma had one of our older cousins come to baby- sit us while she went out. She put her trust in him, at the time I was eight years old. Everything seemed to be all right until we went to bed.

There were two bedrooms, momma slept in the bedroom off the living room and we slept in the second bedroom adjacent to hers. The bedrooms were not that big.

We had a full size bed. Sheree slept in front because it would be easier for her to get up, if she needed too, then Marsha and I slept in the back. I slept behind Marsha against the wall.

After we fell asleep, during the night our cousin came in our room. He called my name in a whisper voice but I pretended not to hear him. He reached over, picked me up anyway, carried me into the living room with him, and laid me on the couch where he was sleeping.

STAINED by HIS BLOOD

He laid me on top of him and, started fondling me, and pressing his body against mines and kissing me with his lips and tongue (yuck). I kept my eyes closed repeating, "I want to go back to bed…"

After repeating these words, he did carry me back to bed. I did not go right to sleep but eventually I did fall asleep, *where was my dad and where was God? The* next morning mom was home and he was gone. We got up and went to school. I never shared with anyone what happen until I was grown. I was embarrassed and ashamed; spirit *of low self-esteem grew within.*

Around Christmas time momma could not afford to buy the three of us girls individual presents so, she asked us what we wanted for Christmas. Of course, being girls, we wanted a doll named "Thumbelina". We were happy with our one shared gift because we thought that we would receive more gifts from other family members at Big Momma's house for Christmas Dinner.

STAINED by HIS BLOOD

Later that day the family all gathered at Big Momma's house. We might have gotten one other gift.

I do remember that there was one family member giving out gifts to my cousins. Both of my cousins were the only children in their family.

When it came to four of us, that family member said, "It's too many of you to buy gifts for."

I remember thinking, how inconsiderate and cruel to say that to children after giving to the other children in the family, *where was my dad?*

My mom would not have ever done that, she played card games with us, and my cousins for penny candy. She loved children and loved having them around. One day she fixed dinner for us, we had pork chops, rice and biscuits. My two cousins, Elaine and Maria came by, and as usual momma offered them something to eat.

STAINED by HIS BLOOD

I do not know why she did that, it was not as if we had pork chops all the time.

Marsha and I had a whole piece and Sheree and Michael shared half pieces. She said we have enough to share and she cut mines and Marsha's whole piece in half. My mom always shared with others.

We never owned a bike nor did we know how to ride one. Our cousins would ride us on the back of their bikes. After many tries, I finally learned how to ride. I rode one good time when I was in my early teens and rode right into the back of my uncle's car—that was the last time I got on a bike, for a while.

I got my driver's permit in my late teens. My older cousin Flamond took me out to a park to teach me how to drive. The park had a gated fence around it because it had a pool inside of it.

Two of my cousins were "back-seat" passengers. They came along to encourage me; at least that was what I thought.

I talked my way through the whole routine. Of course, this conversation took place in my mind where no one could hear me.

Everything started out okay. I turned the ignition to get the car started—*this was good*. Next, I shifted the gear into drive and pressed down on the accelerator a little bit. *"Good, good,"* I said to myself. The car started to move slowly and I was on my way.... As I drove forward, it started to rain lightly.

Flamond asked me to stop, which I did. "That was good," he said. "Now go forward." About this time, my cousins were in the back seat shouting and laughing. I shifted gears into reverse without realizing it. There were too many distractions from the back seat (*peanut gallery*)!

STAINED by HIS BLOOD

I thought I had it all under control but I panicked with all the *"hee hawing"* noise from the back seat.

We were driving toward the gated pool and I did not know how to swim.

Well, Flamond pulled the emergency brakes just in time. Everyone in the car became silent. He and my cousins were so shaken up that, he never committed to taking me out driving again. I was so nervous; I could have wet my pants.

Note: *When going out to drive on a permit for the very first time, do not take an audience! If you do, make sure that they are the quiet-type.*

Well, driving was not on the top of my list for a while. I did get my driver's license later and only had to take the driving test once.

NOTES

CHAPTER 2

Humble Beginnings

STAINED by HIS BLOOD

Later on we moved less than a mile away from our first home. Times were still hard and food was low. Big Momma and my aunts helped us out as much as they could especially whenever we were low on food. I remember the times when momma could not pay our heating bills. She would put our mattresses on the living room floor and set a double burner hot plate in the middle with a pot of water on it to keep us warm. Momma cooked our food on the hot plate because the gas and electricity were off. Momma used an extension cord from the hot plate and plugged it into the outlet in the outside hallway. She also plugged the lamp into the outlet so that we would have lights.

We kept our food, such as eggs and milk on the window ledge out on the back porch, so that they could stay cold. We kept bread and boxed foods covered in plastic containers so the rats and bugs would not have a feast. Mom had us sleep in our clothes at night to keep us even warmer.

STAINED by HIS BLOOD

The next morning, momma would boil water so that we could wash up and change clothes for school. I never had the best of clothing but I wore what momma could afford. She shopped most of the time at a second hand store. I wore funny looking granny shoes; this was not the generation for pointed toe shoes nor was it one for my afro-puff ponytails at least the other children did not think so and yes, kids picked on me and talked about me because of the clothes that my mom thought were ok, well, this was all she could afford.

I was beat up and chased home by a girl one day and then by a boy on another day. What a week! Momma approached the boy and the girl and they both had the same lie for jumping on me—"She's ugly and she started it"! (The devil is such a liar). He will use children and adults to insult you verbally, and to attack you physically. Some people want to fight and will use any excuse to do so because, they are not happy with themselves.

STAINED by HIS BLOOD

Unfortunately, I did not know God at this time nor did I know about the tricks of the enemy. I was quiet and most of the time I stayed to myself. Being a dark complexion girl and unable to dress in the best clothes, I was targeted to be called many names. Momma threatened me saying, she would whip me if I let another person beat me up. I understood that, but the problem was deeper than that. I was afraid and about this time, I had very low self-esteem.

Note: Christians are to fight the good fight of faith and not one another. **1Timothy 6:12 says Fight the good fight of faith, lay hold on eternal life, whereunto thou art also called, and hast professed a good profession before many witnesses.** *We can use words to inflict pain, but we are to use words to help or encourage someone so that we will have peace not only within ourselves but also with others.*

Romans 12:18 says, If it be possible, as much as lieth in you, live peaceably with all men.

STAINED by HIS BLOOD

Some kids pretended to be my friend when I had candy but, when the candy was gone, so were they. I had one friend who I thought was very nice and liked me. We were in fourth grade together. The kids teased her about her weight. Yvonne lived across the street from me. We walked home and played together. She had a little brother and I had a little sister that went to school with us, we picked them up after school together. It was nice having someone to walk and talk with.

Well, that relationship did not last long; it ended when my friend moved away that following summer. Seventh and eighth grade brought me a new friend. We took most of our classes together, including modern dance.

Mom received money and food assistance from the state each month to take care of us. Our neighbors and friends ridiculed her for it. Children heard their parents and other adults discussing our finances.

STAINED by HIS BLOOD

While I was in my gym class, my friend and I stood by our gym teacher. He started talking and predicting different students' future.

He turned toward my friend and me and compared my upbringing with hers, no comparison she had a dad in her home. He said this while looking at her *"You are well dressed and neat, live in a home with a mother and father"* (satan's *set up to destroy me*).

Oh boy, here it comes! Then he said still looking at her but talking about me as if I was not there *"she will end up on welfare like her mother with a house full of children, no husband, and she will not finish high school and the cycle would continue on from generation to generation"*.

I remember thinking, *"OUCH!—that hurt!"* I looked down at myself – my clothes were not the best nor were my shoes.

STAINED by HIS BLOOD

My mother was on welfare and we did have some hard times. We did not have enough money to keep the gas and electricity on most of the time. Sometimes there was not enough food to last us each month but she was a good mother and she was there raising us to be good children in spite of hard times, I loved her anyway.

After hearing my teacher's "predictions", I was determined to prove him wrong...although I was not at times one hundred percent sure that I could, but I was going to try.

Those words pierced my heart and they really did hurt. I did not know how to get them out of my head they just stayed there and then went to my heart and grew.

STAINED by HIS BLOOD

I decided that I could not take life anymore! I was tired of living in poverty and tired of hearing bad things about me and my family. I saw myself as nothing. I did not like me, let alone love me. *Low self-esteem – you think*!

Therefore, I decided that I was going to take some capsules and end my life. It did not matter what type of pills they were, I was determined to take the entire bottle! Anything would do to stop the hurt.

Whatever I found in the medicine cabinet would do the job to kill all the pain I was feeling, I wanted out!

As I stood in front of the bathroom mirror attempting to open the bottle, I heard a voice. *I thought I was in the bathroom alone*...I turned and looked around but somehow I knew it was God.

STAINED by HIS BLOOD

A voice I heard saying this, *"What would your mother do without you? Who would help her with your sisters and brother?"* I thought to myself, "Oh My God! You are God! You can do it! Do It!—You Made Them Too, What Do You Want With Me? Why Do You Even Care?

I did not take the pills (born for his purpose). I am glad I did not plant that suicidal seed. Hallelujah!

NOTES

CHAPTER 3

Transition and Restoration

STAINED by HIS BLOOD

In 1979, I was finishing my sophomore year in high school. At this time, I was fifteen years old and had been on the honor roll for a year and a half. At sixteen, I got a part-time job working as a cashier and salesperson in a hosiery shop and I was glad that I could finally help mom with the bills.

During that time, Marsha was preparing to graduate from eighth grade. She was not feeling well and had gone to the doctor a couple of times. Later on, I found out about my sister's health. One day Marsha came home from the hospital still not feeling well. The doctors could not do anything else for her. Marsha started to lose weight and she cried because her stomach hurt. She went into the hospital again but she was in good spirits. I spoke with her that night and told her all about my new job. I told her when I got paid I was going to buy her a new pair of shoes. I also told her about my new boyfriend Robert Oliver.

Marsha died the following morning. She died from Leukemia (Cancer). I remember seeing my mother's face when she came home that morning from the hospital. She said to me, "Marsha is dead." ...that was one of the saddest days of our lives. The news about her passing affected her classmates greatly. I was sad and hurt – Marsha was my "running buddy" and she helped me with the youngest two and she helped me keep the house, and we both helped momma. There would be no more pillow fights, no more arguing about her wearing my clothes. I could not even cry.

I was always the strong one and I knew I had to be strong for my mother and other family members, or at least that is what I thought.

STAINED by HIS BLOOD

I shed some tears in private the morning of the funeral while I was getting dressed. The funeral was crowded with young people; most of them attended school with Marsha but one of her best friends Latanya, did not have the strength to attend the funeral because she was so sad and could not understand why Marsha died. Our dad was at the funeral. I do not know what he was thinking but I was angry with him for not being there for us, for Marsha. While she was in the hospital, Marsha asked about him but we had no way of contacting him. Momma tried but somehow he got the news a little too late.

I knew that Marsha was not lying in the casket, even though it looked kind of, like her, "she" was not there. She was with God, still living and smiling, without pain, 2Corinthians 5:8 says, **We are confident, I say, and willing rather to be absent from the body, and to be present with the Lord.** I guess somewhere in my spirit I knew this.

STAINED by HIS BLOOD

The thought of Marsha with God carried me through the funeral.

...I only have one picture of my sister. It is a good picture where she was wearing my sweater and my earrings—*"in my stuff again."*

Before Marsha passed, she was able to attend her eighth grade graduation although she was weak, she was determined to attend. I am so glad she did because she really deserved it. She was a good student.

One night I had a dream about Marsha. Marsha, and I, and some other kids from the neighborhood were sitting on our front porch the way we use to. Well, Marsha kept getting up off the porch to leave so I kept grabbing her to make her sit down. I told her to save her strength so she would not get tired or sick but she would not stay. *The dream meant let go— she is okay and she does not want to stay here or come back.*

STAINED by HIS BLOOD

Heaven must be some kind of place, I mean, living with God. I do not think there are any words to describe it because 'sister girl' would not listen to me! Nope, Marsha would not stay with me. It became apparent that she had somewhere to go. Her spirit was at peace. Knowing this, I let go and had a peace within my heart. Thank you Lord.

And the peace of God, which passeth all understanding, shall keep your hearts and mind through Christ Jesus Phil. 4:7.

God carried our mother through this difficult time. He gave her strength, His strength from the beginning to the end. That was a lot for her, as a single parent, to deal with alone—but she did it for the rest of us.

My mother, Daisy M. Peoples, "you were and still are one of a kind and I thank God for you. You are one of God's best, a mother like no other".

Restoration

After Marsha went home to be with the Lord, daddy became a part of my life again. The relationship was hard at first.... I had gone through eight years without him but I allowed him back into my life because I needed to—besides, he would always be my earthly father and that would never change. I believe I needed that relationship with him as much as he needed it with me. It took some time. We had to start from where we were and not look back into the past because we could not make up for what had already happened.

Walking in forgiveness is one of the keys to unlocking healing, prosperity etc. Unforgiveness will hinder your prayers from being answered. **Mark 11:25-26 says, And when you stand praying, forgive, if you have ought against any: that our Father also which is in heaven may forgive you your trespasses but if you do not forgive, neither will your father which is in heaven forgive your trespasses.** This is true, if we do not forgive others, our heavenly father will not forgive us. You have opened yourself up to attacks from the enemy when you do not forgive. Once you step out from under the umbrella of God's protection, this will open a door for the enemy to come after you even more. Ask God to help you if you have a hard time with this.

STAINED by HIS BLOOD

NOTES

CHAPTER 4

Desires

Determination

While attending grade school and high school there were a number of students having babies. I remember how hard it was for my mother and as a result, I was determined that I was going to finish high school and go to college. After college, I planned to have a "fairytale wedding" and a husband that would love me as much as I loved him, maybe even more. I was a Christian and I wanted a Christian husband as well. Yes!—I prayed for these things. I finished high school and wanted to go to college but I did not have the finances to attend so I decided to work full time at the hosiery shop for a year.

Housing

I moved into a basement apartment with Big Momma. She moved into the basement apartment because my aunt got married and she moved out from the second floor of my uncle and aunt's building. Big Momma could no longer afford the rent living by herself. My uncle and aunt lived in the basement apartment they moved out and onto the first floor. My grandmother figured it would be easier for her to live in the basement apartment—the rent was certainly cheaper. One day, Big Momma and I had a discussion about how nice it would be if we could all live together in the upstairs apartment. There was plenty of room for Big Momma, momma, Sheree, Michael and me—I used to dream about all of the benefits....

STAINED by HIS BLOOD

We would have a washer and dryer because Big-Momma had both. With our combined incomes, we could afford the rent. I told Big Momma how nice it would be if the people upstairs were to move out. One morning they did and we all moved in that evening! It was a thought.

God was listening to our conversation because only He could have made this happen within 24 hours! We were all together for only a short time though. A year or so later momma moved into another apartment with a friend.

STAINED by HIS BLOOD

When I was about sixteen years old, I joined a church by the name of First Corinthians Missionary Baptist Church and I sang in the choir for eight or nine years. I remember sometimes when the choir would minister at other churches the young women in the choir gathered around the mirrors to fix their make-up and hair while I sat off to the side where I applied my make-up, and fixed my hair. I did not want to look into a mirror. At times, I would pass by a mirror and would never look in it *(spirit of low self-esteem still there)*. Back then, I still did not know how to get rid of it, this thing, this spirit; I did not even know what it was, and why I felt this way.

STAINED by HIS BLOOD

Even as a "saved" teenager, I was a fan of a Pop Rock Star and I attended his concerts when the opportunity presented itself. I was eighteen or nineteen years old when I attended my last concert. I remember him singing and all these super fans were crying and fainting over him (mostly females). I thought to myself, *"he is not doing anything but singing a love ballad and girls are fainting and dropping like flies"*. At that moment, I could not believe that I used to cry over him. He did not even know me but *Jesus knew my name*. He was not God, at least not the One, True and Living God that I came to know. How many of these fans would come to see Jesus?

Crowds seem to flock to non-Christian singing groups where the band members do not care if your soul is lost in hell. I thought, *"What a waste of my time."* No human being could have done what Jesus did on the cross for me; died for me and was raised up on the third day with all power in His hands.

STAINED by HIS BLOOD

So that *we* could have eternal life John 3:16 says, **For God so loved the world, that he gave his only begotten Son, that whosoever believeth in him should not perish, but have everlasting life.**

My eyes were opened spiritually and all I could think about was, *"what am I doing here?"* In the midst of the concert, I began to say a prayer quietly; with all the music, no one could hear me anyway.

"Lord forgive me, I did not know I had made a god out of this rock singer and now I feel so out of place being here. Lord I thank you for opening my eyes so that I could see how much of a deceiver the enemy is. Please help those around me who are also being deceived and are not saved."

STAINED by HIS BLOOD

It took me two years before I could enroll in a two-year business college. I majored in Travel Management. One or two classes short of a degree I learned that I needed $800 to graduate. The financial aid officer suggested that I get the money from my parents. I remember telling her, "My parents don't have that kind of money...if we had that type of money it would not have taken me two years to start college after graduating from high school."

I realize that $800 really was not a lot of money but at that time, we did not have it. Well, I did not graduate but I continued to work and help momma with the bills. I later worked for a bookstore at O'Hare Airport as a cashier/salesperson. While working there, I continued to look for a career in the travel field without my degree.

STAINED by HIS BLOOD

I knew that God said He would give me the desires of my heart if I delight myself in Him just like Psalm 37:4 tells me, **Delight** *yourself also in the* LORD; *and he shall give thee the desires of thine heart.*

NOTES

CHAPTER 5

Two Becoming One

Engaged...Wedding

Robert and I were still dating in 1987. We talked about marriage, and we even settled on names for our children Ebonee and Robert, Jr. In the fall of 1987 Robert asked me to marry him. The proposal was romantic because I did not expect it. At the time, I said yes but I still had to talk to God about this. I wanted to make sure Robert was the man that God had chosen for me, and that I was the woman God had chosen for him. God knew our future better than we did.

God also knew we would be able to overcome difficult situations if we kept Him first. In order to play it safe, we decided to seek God and not make such an important decision based solely on our feelings during that moment.

As I continued to pray and read God's Word, I received an 'okay' through a dream. In the dream, I was walking down the aisle and when I got to the front and turn to look at my groom, it was Robert. There was an indescribable peace. It over shadowed not just me but the place where we were getting married at, my church. Therefore, we began to plan our wedding and everything else fell into place. I loved Robert and thought what our marriage or family would be like. What could I do or give him that he never had besides me being his wife. He had two girls already from previous relationships. God whispered to me "a *son he does not have a son*". You are right, a son we had hoped to have one; I guess I did not really look at it that way or how important that would be to him. Thank you Lord.

God's Way or NO WAY!

Okay readers, while I am planning a wedding let us go back a little.... My mother has taught me many lessons. One of her statements that stayed with me was, *"Always have respect for yourself"*. I remembered those words when Robert asked me to live with him some years before he asked me to marry him. I answered, "No!" I told him, "If I'm good enough to live with you, I know that I am good enough for you to marry." Let us make this legal according to the Word of God—*papers please!* We dated 9 years off and on. During those years, I do remember leaning on him a lot for my happiness actually, a little too much.

I realized later that I was special, not because a man thought that I was, or told me that I was, but because God made me special and unique.

Psalm 139:14 says, "**I will praise thee; for I am fearfully and wonderfully made**".

STAINED by HIS BLOOD

God loves me; I am the apple of his eye. He expressed His love with every drop of blood that Jesus shed on the cross, through every pain he felt and with every stripe that He endured. While hanging on that cross, Jesus did not complain. Instead, He remembered how very much He loves me, Mareen! *Yes! I do see the cross as a personal act of love—don't you?* God showed His love for me on the cross and I wanted to show my love for Him, let Him know that He was (and is) first in my life.

Because of that, I did not move in with Robert.

Proverbs 31:10, 30 says, Who can find a virtuous woman? for her price is far above rubies. Favour is deceitful, and beauty is vain: but a woman that feareth the Lord, she shall be praised.

Well, let us go back to the wedding that Robert and I planned....

STAINED by HIS BLOOD

The wedding was scheduled to start at 5p.m. on August 6, 1988. The wedding started around 6:50 that night. Can you believe that? No, it was not me I was ready. I sat for so long that my gown had creases that looked as if they were sewn into the dress. The wedding was delayed (late) for almost two hours because the flower girls' dresses were still being sewn and Robert forgot the marriage license and my wedding band. In the end, we used my engagement ring and a ring from Robert's aunt. Wow! It took us a year to plan the wedding and reception and it was all over in about three hours and was worth it.

STAINED by HIS BLOOD

We had a beautiful wedding with colors of royal blue and fuchsia. There were twelve bridesmaids and twelve groomsmen, two best men, one maid of honor, one matron of honor, five flower girls, one ring bearer and over three hundred family and friends to share August 6, 1988 with us—thank you Jesus.

The day after the wedding, I woke up and felt a little uncomfortable. As I looked around the room, I realized that I was going to spend the rest of my life as a married woman in a different place other than with my family. Now do not get me wrong, I *wanted* to be married. Life just felt a little different...and yet wonderful at the same time.

Reality Sets In

That next day after the wedding, I went over to my moms' to pick up some of my things. Momma and Big Momma were walking around in their robes looking gloomy.

All the lights were off, and they looked like someone had died. I asked what was wrong and mom said, "You left us, you don't live here with us anymore."

She tried to put on a sad face as she spoke but it did not last very long. She started laughing and said, "You can give your keys back to me since you won't need them anymore. You are now the responsibility of your husband and you have your own place now with your husband.

In other words, *he is* responsible for taking care of you. Well, I just knew she was kidding about the keys so I kept my keys!

STAINED by HIS BLOOD

Robert and I agreed that our marriage should not be serious all of the time. What we meant was that it was okay to laugh with each other as we did while dating, why change that? I think we laugh even more now that we are married.

One night during the first few weeks of being married, I could not sleep but Robert was sleeping quite well. I decided to polish my nails. I was still not sleepy so I decided to do his toenails and the color was red! He was sleeping so sound that he could not feel a thing. I laughed quietly as I was doing this; it was so funny to me, and afterwards, I felt very sleepy and then I drifted off to sleep.

I slept so well that I did not hear him when he got up and then suddenly I heard him call me, *"Mareen!"* I woke up in a rush and immediately remembered what I had done. He stormed out of the bathroom with the towel wrapped around his waist fussing-but-laughing at the same time.

STAINED by HIS BLOOD

He said, *"If I had gone down to the gym and got ready to take my shower, can you imagine? The guys would not have understood that my wife was bored and decided to polish my toe nails red!"* We laughed a long time on that one.

I remember another incident that happened during our first year of marriage. At the time, I worked for a temporary agency while continuing to search for employment in the travel field. We lived on the eighth floor of an apartment building on the west side of Chicago.

STAINED by HIS BLOOD

I came home from work one hot evening and noticed that Robert was not at the door to greet me. I knew that he was home because our car was parked out front. I wondered where he was and what was he doing. I proceeded toward the bedroom in order to change my clothes. As I walked past the kitchen going toward the bedroom, I heard a noise.

I stopped and peeked into the kitchen and there was a naked chicken (which was 'supposed' to be cooked for dinner) just sitting there on the counter with its legs crossed and its arms flapping. It said, *"how was your day Mrs. Oliver?"* I responded with laughter and replied, *"Okay."* Well, the chicken then decided to do a dance for me on the counter. You should have seen this chicken dance; its legs and arms went this way and that way. I laughed so hard that afternoon, and it was exactly what I needed. My husband managed to make a puppet out of our dinner—he has such a great sense of humor.

STAINED by HIS BLOOD

I began to increase my pursuit of a career in travel when the temporary employment agency could no longer provide consistent work. Our finances were a little low so I committed to go job searching every morning. One day, as I was coming in from searching, I remember talking to God. I told Him about having to walk in the northwestern suburbs where there were no sidewalks; I had to walk in the streets and wait for the bus while standing in the grass. As far as I was concerned, it was impossible to wait for a suburban bus to come because it had a schedule of its own, an every hour or more for the wait. In addition, this was during the winter months and it was quite cold standing in one place.

I wore the same black shoes every time I went out and every day when I got home, I tossed those shoes across the room and told my Father God that I was not going back out there! It was too cold to walk around in heels and a skirt and wait on buses.

STAINED by HIS BLOOD

A word of advice, NEVER tell the Father what you are not going to do because He has a sense of humor (where do you think His children got it from). The following morning I could not even sleep late—there God was, waking me up early and there I was (again), going on group interviews with different airlines!

I attended many group interviews, this time I knew what to say and what not to say. I was called for a second interview with an airline for the first time.

I was not overly excited because I had been through this routine before. However, when I was called for a third interview I thought, "Wow, this is new for me."

I went into the interview with a positive attitude. There was only one interviewer and I thought it was going well until, I was asked a strange question.

STAINED by HIS BLOOD

"Who helped you with your resume?" I thought, what does this have to do with the position I am applying for? So, I asked, "Why, is there a problem?" He replied, "*No it is good*" and started to laugh. He asked me about the resume again. "No one," I replied again, what was with this person?

I left the interview feeling very low and confused. That night I tossed, turned, and could not fall asleep. My resume was great – and how could it not be with the help of the Holy Spirit? God then explained to me that I had not done or said anything wrong. God continued to explain that the interviewer has a prejudice spirit. He concluded by encouraging me not to worry about a job with that company because that was not the job He had for me. Well, back to job searching again....

After several interviews with TWA, I was hired. Thank you Lord! The training was difficult for me but God had a vessel who worked at TWA to serve as my instructor.

She began to encourage me each step of the way, we attended the same church. It turned out that my instructor was the Pastor's daughter—Donna.

Only God could have arranged such a partnership. I remember my instructor telling me to "Trust God and know that I can do all things through Christ who strengthens me." One Sunday morning my instructor prayed with me and asked God to give me wisdom and to open my understanding and you know He did! I successfully completed the training and then worked as a Reservations Agent for TWA. I became an agent without a degree in travel. God is almighty...He is my God.

NOTES

CHAPTER 6

My Name Is Ebonee

STAINED by HIS BLOOD

Psalm 127:3 says, Lo, children are an heritage of the Lord: and the fruit of the womb is his reward.

Three years into the marriage, Robert and I were still growing as one. We had some rough times, we disagreed at times I packed up and left about three times and the last time he just looked at me and said just leave my basketball. We had a lot of growing to do. I remembering asking God to help me be the wife He called me to be to him, and for him the husband you called him to be to me. We shared our thoughts, our feelings, our past and our dreams.

In fact, we shared many things with one another just before we got marriage. Such as, what kind of dishwashing liquid we would use, a matter of fact that was one of our first disagreement, and it was in the grocery store, choosing a dishwashing detergent.

STAINED by HIS BLOOD

I thought we had settled this beforehand. I do not know why there was a disagreement since I was going to be the one doing the dishes most of the time anyway. Although we had more of a "friendship" relationship the year before we got married; I think we became best friends during our marriage. It took a lot of work, patience, disagreements (arguments), trust and prayer. We prayed for God's help, even when we did not want to pray.

We were stuck together for life because we had decided on it. Anyway as I was saying before, after 3years into our marriage Robert and I decided we wanted to start a family so we decided on the day we would conceive. We had a candle light dinner and ordered a cake with pink and blue icing because we did not know if our first-born would be Ebonee or Robert Jr.

STAINED by HIS BLOOD

I did not have a taste for meat in my first three months of pregnancy. I remember coming home with some groceries and Robert was putting them away, while he was putting them away he noticed that I did not buy any meat. He said "Honey, where is the meat?" I explained as I was walking through the store the smell of meat just did not agree with my stomach. So, I got all fruits and vegetables and I suggested that he might want to go out to the store and get it until my taste buds for meat returned and it did after three months. During the first three months, my blood pressure was high. As a result, I had to take an early maternity leave in my third month.

During the last three or four months of my pregnancy I experienced back pain, fatigue and swelling in the feet somewhat normal for some pregnant women.

STAINED by HIS BLOOD

During my last trimester, I just did not want to be pregnant anymore. I wanted my baby to come right then.

I wanted my figure back. I wanted my body back, literally and figuratively speaking I think I was just tired. Tired of the weight which was not much but I still had to find clothes to wear and shoes that would fit my swollen feet.

It was frustrating trying to find clothes to fix during the last couple of months in 90-degree weather. My husband did not know what to say to me or how to make me feel more comfortable. He pampered me a bit more to keep me happy, which made things a little easier for me.

One day Robert and I attended a funeral. There was no air conditioning in the church and it was hot inside so I decided to stand in the cooler air outside.

STAINED by HIS BLOOD

Robert came out to stand with me and an evangelist walked up to me and prophesied that I was going to have a beautiful baby girl. I told her, *"I don't think so!"* What an attitude I had.

That was not nice, but I did not receive it because everyone else was always trying to tell me what I was going to have based on the "way" my stomach was sitting. Some said if your stomach sits high then it would be a boy. Others said it would be a girl I simply did not believe any predictions.

Besides, I thought a boy would be great but on the other hand I was a first child and I was a good big sister. I decided to leave it in the Lord's hands. The day before I went into labor Robert fixed dinner, he prepared tacos I told him I wanted mine spicy because I was going into labor that night and after the baby comes, I would be nursing and would not be able to eat any spicy food.

STAINED by HIS BLOOD

Later that night I laid down, Robert decided he was going to go out for a little while. I was not pleased with that because I would be going into labor anytime soon. He said he would be back soon and I replied ok, but if I go into labor while you are still out, I was just going to call my daddy (his father). As I was sleeping I was awaken by a soft pop sound and then I felt wetness Wow! My water had broken I sat up and there was Robert sitting on the floor next to the bed asleep.

I was sleeping pretty well because I did not notice when he came in. I nudged him and said its time! he responded in a sleepy voice, time for what? I could not believe it! All this time we were waiting to say this, and he responded "for what?"

We got to the hospital and settled in our room and the pain was mild. Robert stood by holding my hand, I laughed with the nurses for a while suddenly I did not want to laugh or smile anymore.

STAINED by HIS BLOOD

The contractions started coming and the doctor wanted to examine me to find out how many centimeters I was. Are you kidding me! I thought to myself, as I responded, No! It was too painful for that! He looked at my husband and told him "tell your wife I need to examine her" as if I was coherent or something, I was just in a lot of pain. I allowed him to check me. He responded, "Okay she's about 7 centimeters the baby will be coming soon".

Robert said, "I wish that I could help, is there anything that I can do for you?" I replied, "No, just sit down next to me...and I do not want you to hold my hand anymore right now." I did not want to talk to the nurses nor did I want them to rub me or touch me anymore. They gave me a shot of medicine for the pain, I fell asleep and after some hours passed, I was awakened by even harder pain.

STAINED by HIS BLOOD

The medicine had worn off. I thought to myself *Jesus took all pain but he forgot this one.* They were double contractions back to back no relief. At this point, I was not a pretty person. Robert and some of the doctors were in my room watching a game. Robert was talking about our nephew who at the time was playing professional ball. Well at this point I could care less about the game or my nephew's profession, although, I love him very much but, I just could not understand them talking about basketball at a time that I was in so much pain in the same room. The pain came back to back, no time to inhale or exhale. I thought about momma and big momma they survived this and so would I. The doctor came over to me after seventeen hours of labor and said, "Mrs. Oliver, I think you have suffered enough, we're going to give you a cesarean because the baby has not dropped, because your birth canal is not big enough for the baby to come through".

STAINED by HIS BLOOD

"Okay," I replied. "Is that necessary?" Robert asked. I looked over at him and thought to myself, because I was in too much pain to respond to his question aloud. *'What does he mean is that necessary? Let him lie here for seventeen hours—he wouldn't make it!' God did not make man to endure this kind of pain nor have a baby, impossible".*

There was a curtain drawn across me from the neck down so that we could not see what the doctor was doing. However, the doctor walked us through every step that he was taking. Towards the end, as the doctor was pulling Ebonee out of her comfort, Robert decided he wanted to look over the curtain. "NO!" I shouted I did not think this was a good idea. Well, Ebonee was born with her eyes open wide and looking around. Robert held her first and then brought her over to me. I just cried tears of joy and thought, *"what a mighty God we serve that He would give us such a precious little life to be responsible for".*

STAINED by HIS BLOOD

John 16:21 says, A woman when she is in travail hath sorrow, because her hour is come: but as soon as she is delivered of the child, she remembereth no more the anguish, for joy that a man is born into the world.

As the doctor completed the surgery, I found that I was tired and still drowsy from the drugs so I drifted off to sleep....

When I woke up, my legs were propped up, and crossed. I did not know how or when I did that. (my mom said I use to sleep this way all the time and she would knock my legs down, I remember vaguely). I asked the nurse, "Are those my legs?" I was still numb from the stomach down. *"Yes, Mrs. Oliver,"* she replied. I then asked her, "How long have they been propped up like that and when is the feeling going to come back?" ...I guess she did not know how long my legs were crossed. She replied, *"The feeling will come back soon."*

I started thinking about how some people, are paralyzed, from the waist down and how grateful I am to know that the feelings in my legs would return.

During the nine months that I carried Ebonee, Robert and I talked to her. We told her who she "was" and what she "was" going to be in Christ. According to Romans 4:17, we were **calling things that be not as though they were.** We told her that Jesus Christ loves her and that she would speak out boldly for Him as He gave her Words.

Proverbs 22:6 says, **Train up a child in the way he should go: and when he is old, he will not depart from it.**

She would know that she had power to do ALL things through Christ. This is what Philippians 4:13 tells us, **I can do all things through Christ which strengtheneth me.**

STAINED by HIS BLOOD

We also spoke words into her about the kind of man that she would marry; a man after God's own heart – the man that God would send her. We prayed that all our children would marry saved spouses. We remained in the hospital for five days because my blood cell count was low.

The doctors had run several tests in order to find out the cause. I just wanted to have my baby and go home so I said, "Lord, fix it please!" And wouldn't you know it He fixed it! My blood cell count increased and we were released to go home.

In my early days of motherhood, I asked God to help me to be a good mother just as I had asked Him to help me be a good wife. I had decided to nurse Ebonee because, I knew that waking up in the wee hours of the morning to warm a bottle was not for me, and that the breast milk would be better for her anyway. Apparently, it was God's way of feeding his babies. God, our Father, has provided our bodies with the milk for the little lives that He give us.

STAINED by HIS BLOOD

It is just like God to give you something as precious as a baby and then provide food for that baby. You have a choice to use baby formula or breast milk, the breast milk is free and it comes in abundance, no lack, no side effects. Wow! He loves us.

God is great! It just makes me smile when I think about how Great He Is and that He is my father, my daddy God.

After ten weeks, I returned to work and it was rough. I worked from 3pm to 11 p.m. I did this for about three weeks.

My work hours then changed from 7am to 3pm with weekends off. I pumped milk during my breaks. Robert would take me to work every morning and drop Ebonee off at my mothers' and return home to sleep for an hour or two and then head off to work.

I took the bus to my mother's house to pick up Ebonee and from there I either took a cab home or walked around the corner to my in-laws house.

STAINED by HIS BLOOD

"My daddy," as I called my father-in-law, would bring us home most of the time. I did have my driver's license.

A couple of friends taught me how to drive and Robert took me to get my license after we got married. Robert gave me my first car and I drove that car everywhere I needed to go until it died. Unfortunately, it died right before Ebonee was born. Robert's parents (James, Sr. and Everett Oliver) are the kindest people you could ever know. They were willing to help us as well as anyone else who may have needed their help.

We are to help one another and not just the body of Christ. We are to help all people – after all, God freely helps us. That is how God drew us to Him, using His unconditional love? Real love, just like when He gave His only begotten Son Jesus".

STAINED by HIS BLOOD

John 3:16* says, *For God so loved the world, that he gave his only begotten Son, that whosoever believeth in him should not perish, but have everlasting life.

Ebonee learned how to walk the day after her first birthday. I dropped her off at her Godparents house (Rodney and Marilyn Ward, Sr.) so that I could go to the store. She took off walking toward the door to come after me.

Miss Ebonee walked so much that I had to put her in a walker in order for me to keep up with her!

One day, we were in the house and Ebonee was in her walker.

I was doing something in the bedroom and all of a sudden, I saw my baby take off running to the front door so fast, I had never seen her move so quickly.

STAINED by HIS BLOOD

The front door opened and there was her daddy. She had heard his keys rattling as he came up the stairs. Definitely a "daddy's girl" and she still is today just as her two sisters Tanisha and Brandy are also. When he would pick her up, she would just fall out in his arms.

NOTES

CHAPTER 7

Second Opinion Please?

STAINED by HIS BLOOD

In 1994, I noticed that my menstrual cycle had not come for a couple of months. I took numerous pregnancy tests and they all came back negative; and yet the doctors insisted that I was pregnant. I did not agree with their assessments, especially after taking so many pregnancy tests and blood tests. I went to a doctor and told him that I was NOT PREGNANT but that no other doctor would listen to me so, I asked if he would *puh-leeze* take x-rays and find out what was going on.... He listened to me and ordered the x-rays. Well, the x-rays came back and the doctor informed me that I needed a hysterectomy. He said there was a tumor blocking my ovary (not ovaries), and it needed to be removed right away. Robert and I decided to get a second opinion.

The second physician asked me how many children I had and did I want to have any more. I replied, "I have one and yes, I do plan on having more." After he looked over my test results, he informed me that the tumor was the size of a grapefruit, and it needed to be removed. However, he only had to remove the left ovary, meaning, I DID NOT need a hysterectomy – praise God!

The doctor explained that there were two options for removing the tumor. One option was to perform the surgery through my naval, and if that option was not successful, he would remove the tumor by making a "bikini cut" approximately three inches below the naval.

This surgery was similar to a cesarean and I was all too familiar with that kind of procedure. The doctor explained that I would not have to stay in the hospital overnight. Instead, he said I would be able to have the surgery and go home "as long as everything went well."

STAINED by HIS BLOOD

We agreed and set the date for surgery—of course, Robert did take off from work to be with me.

The day of the surgery, we waited forty-five minutes in the doctor's office before I was called in for pre-surgery preparations. Robert waited patiently in the waiting area for me. I changed into one of those funny gowns with the back out – that MUST have been a man's invention and if it was not, what was her name!

I laid down on the table as a nurse took my temperature and then she left me, alone. As I laid there in the cold, I realized that I needed to go to the bathroom. I thought, *'this should be quick, it's not like I have a lot of clothes on.'* I got the nurses attention to let her know where I was going.

STAINED by HIS BLOOD

When I got back to the table and took my position I was alone again, an opportunity to talk to God: *"Lord keep me and give me peace because I am feeling a little uncomfortable lying here...and I am cold. Lord, if you do not keep me, then I will not be kept, at this moment, as it is, my life is in your hands anyway. I trust you to take care of me and bring me through this. I will come through this, and by Jesus' stripes, I am, already healed. Lord, give my husband peace while he is sitting waiting for me in the waiting room Amen."*

The nurse came in and moved me into the operating room. There were doctors bringing in utensils for the surgery...you would think they would have waited until I was unconscious.

STAINED by HIS BLOOD

A nurse came over to me to insert an I.V. and she asked me how I was feeling? I told her, "I would have been better if I had not seen the utensils...why didn't you wait until I was unconscious before you brought them in and—before I could finish fussing the anesthesia knocked me out. —Waking up.

I remember thinking, "Okay, where am I...is the three hour surgery over already...did I make it through? I don't feel any pain". Then I heard a voice that was so wonderful to hear. I heard my husband's voice, as he was talking to the doctor. The nurse called me, and then my husband started calling me "Mrs. Oliver"—what a wonderful sound. I opened my eyes and tried to remove the oxygen mask from my face because it was uncomfortable.

STAINED by HIS BLOOD

It took about six weeks to recover, and then I went back to the doctor for a final physical to make sure that I was healing properly. The doctor explained that the tumor was a fibroid tumor. He said that sometimes women get these things and he said that I did not have a thing to worry about. He said the tumor was not cancerous. "This was another thing that Jesus had taken to the cross along with cancer and high blood pressure".

STAINED by HIS BLOOD

NOTES

CHAPTER 8

Do Not Receive That!

STAINED by HIS BLOOD

I was back to my old routine of being the wife and mother, and it felt great! Robert and I decided to have another child because God had promised us a son. My menstrual cycle was late so, I took some tests, and I was told that I was pregnant. Just to make sure everything was all right, I took more tests and my doctor said he would call me if he needed to see me; in other words, *"if anything was wrong."* Two weeks passed and I had not heard from the doctor so I assumed everything was okay. I continued with my usual routine but I was more aware of what I ate and also avoided any heavy lifting.

STAINED by HIS BLOOD

I decided that I needed a time of revival for more strength, power and a fresh anointing. Therefore, I considered some time alone away from home, housework, and every day duties. God put in my spirit to attend our church's "1994 Annual Women's Retreat".

I still considered changing my mind because I figured we could use the money for something else such as bills (second-guessed what I had heard the Holy Spirit tell me). However, the Holy Spirit used Robert to encourage me to go.

Robert said that I looked like I could use some time away from my everyday routine. I had been in the hospital with Ebonee for a few days because she had pneumonia. He said the retreat would be good for me spiritually and physically.

STAINED by HIS BLOOD

The morning of the retreat, I remembered that God had told me who would be my roommate. When I arrived at the church, I shared what He had told me with that person. Her name was Sharon and she did not question it. In fact, she planned to room with someone else but that person did not show up – this sounded like God's perfect plan! I arrived at the retreat and felt good.

Each class and workshop was about faith. I learned so much, then I remember how I felt before going; I felt drained and my cup was empty. I wanted more and I knew that God had more for me. I knew that I was not going to return home the same way I had left.

STAINED by HIS BLOOD

I wanted to know more about Him; I wanted to have the kind of faith like the woman with the issue of blood for twelve years.

"And, behold, a woman, which was diseased with an issue of blood twelve years, came behind him, and touched the hem of his garment: For she said within herself, If I may but touch his garment, I shall be whole. But Jesus turned him about, and when he saw here, he said, Daughter, be of good comfort; thy faith hath made thee whole. And the woman was made whole from that hour" **Matthew 9:20-22.**

I remember leaving that workshop amazed by what I had heard, her faith made her whole and healed. The speaker taught also taught on Mark 11:23 **"Whatever we ask God for that is in His Word; we can have it according to our faith, if we receive and believe when we pray.**

STAINED by HIS BLOOD

I began to talk to God within myself saying, *"So...whatever I have faith for and believe without a doubt, according to Your Word Lord, You will do or give it to me?—yeah, right! ...okay Lord, prove it!"*

I did not know how He was going to show me. I just wanted to know Him at a different level as the woman with the issue of blood did. I wanted to trust Him like that. I wanted to believe in Him and have faith as she had. I wanted to know Him. I did not know Him to be a Healer in that way. I guess, I mean as far as healing miraculously. I wanted to touch the hem of his garment. I knew Him to come through for me and other ways including surgery but not in a way like this woman did. She trusted him and knew without a doubt that she would be healed.

STAINED by HIS BLOOD

Now, at each workshop, my eyes and ears were opened to receive God's Word. Every word spoken was very important to me. I wanted to know God on a higher and more personal level. I did not know why at the time, I just did.

I had a hunger to know who my God was and who I really was in Him; I wanted to know more about him and the woman with issue of blood as well; I wanted to have that kind of faith in Him that she had; I wanted to trust Him as she did—I wanted to love Him more. After all, how can you trust someone you do not know or whose character you do not understand?

The woman heard that Jesus heals and went to Him to receive her healing. I heard about Jesus being a Healer, However, did I really believe that He was?

STAINED by HIS BLOOD

I wondered why I wanted to know more about Him in the area of healing and why was the Holy Spirit pulling and pushing me towards Jesus, to get in His presence. I knew, from singing in the choir, about Jesus being a Healer and I often told people to trust Jesus but I had to ask myself, *"Do I really believe what I sing and read about in the Bible? If I do believe, to what degree do I believe in His healing power?"*

The second night we were there, we were told to find a space to pray to God. We all gathered into a large room and found our own small space to pray whatever we wanted to pray about, unto God. I found a space in the corner, I started praising God, and suddenly the tears started flowing and did not stop. God showed me in the spirit layers of clothes falling off me. I could not stop crying, each layer carried a bad seed that was planted in my past, a seed that was not planted by God.

Every time I thought, I was finished crying, there was another layer of clothing coming off me. God showed me what each one was for. I did not want to see them because they caused me so much pain and hurt in my past. I just wanted to stop crying and get away from the place He had me in. I wanted to end the crying on my own. Overall, the clothes that were falling off represented different spirits such as low self-esteem and shame. Not all of the clothes represented the things I did that made me ashamed to face, but from words that were said to me and about me, that were buried deep in my heart. Layers upon layers...

Just as I thought I had finished crying, and attempted to walk away, He said "No! One more, I was thinking what? I have no more tears, no more energy to cry. He then showed me my sister Marsha. He said, *"I know you did not grieve for her the way you wanted to, because you thought you had to be strong but now I am freeing you, Do It Now!"*

STAINED by HIS BLOOD

I said "Lord that was over 15 years ago!" I thought like that would make a difference, so what about all the other hurt and pain that was planted over fifthteen years ago. He said, *"Let it go!"*, and all of a sudden, an uncontrollable stream of tears came flowing down, all for her, how I missed her so much! The past hurt, and the pain I kept inside was released. The last of the clothing fell off in the spirit; I had lost so much weight, spiritual weight. I also forgave my male cousin. I returned home feeling refreshed, revived and rested, but also ready to do some research on faith.

I had been saved since I was fourteen. I wanted to know my identity as a Christian. I wanted to know the real Jesus and why the Holy Spirit was leading me in that direction. Therefore, I continued to seek scriptures and materials on faith by reading His Word daily—morning, noon, night and in the midnight hours. In fact, I read every chance I got. It was as if I could never get full.

I went to Bible class, weekly, and the teacher was teaching on faith. Wow, it was just what I wanted! Yes, I am sure I needed it, I mean, to hear teaching on faith…. but this was different I wanted it! I wanted God!

A week or two after returning home from the retreat I decided to call my doctor to find out about my ultra sound. I wanted to know if the baby was okay and find out when I needed to come in for my next visit. I assumed the test results were good since the doctor had not called me back in a couple of weeks....

NOTES

CHAPTER 9

I Have The Victory!

STAINED by HIS BLOOD

"Hello doctor, I called to find out about my ultrasound." *"Mrs. Oliver, it doesn't look good, you should have been in my office long before now."* "You told me you were going to call me about my test results but you did not, I had to call you. What are you trying to tell me?"

The doctor paused for a second or two and then continued, *"You are not pregnant—I need you to come to my office."* "Why? What do you need me to come in for? NO! I am not coming there. What do you have to tell me, you can tell me now". *"I need for you to come into the office."* "NO, tell me what you need to tell me now!"

"We could try to help you get pregnant but we would rather try to get you to live for another ten to fifteen years...." I thought to myself, is he trying to tell me that I am dying? Is that what he is saying? THAT IS what he is *saying*. *"I need for you to come into the office."*

"NO, tell me now. I want to know, I'm at home...."
"Your right ovary does not look good; it has tumors all around it. You might need another operation to remove them—a hysterectomy...Mrs. Oliver, depending on what is more important to you, 'your' life or 'a baby'...we CAN get you pregnant but we would rather give you life."

"I don't want to talk to you, you are scaring me (fear tried to take over so that I could not hear God) I hung up! Then, the Holy Spirit immediately started talking to me. He reminded me of all that I had learned over the past week. He comforted me with these words, **"Know who you are in Christ. Call the doctor back now!**

"...Okay doctor tell me what you have to tell me, what is my next step?" *"You need to see a cancer specialist."* "So you can't do anything for me?" I was still in shock, wondering if this was really happening to me.

The doctor said, *"no, but I will set up an appointment for you to see the cancer specialist. I will call you back in a week with your appointment date because it takes at least a week to even get an appointment."*

"I thought to myself, 'HE IS TELLING ME THAT I AM DYING AND HE WANTS ME TO WAIT TO HEAR FROM HIM IN A WEEK?' "What do I do now? How do I function from now until next week; seven WHOLE days...is he nuts?" God then spoke to me and said, **"But the Comforter, which is the Holy Spirit, whom the Father will send in my name, He shall teach you all things and bring all things to your remembrance, whatsoever I have said unto you" (John 14:26).**

I wondered, 'What do I need to remember, and how is He going to help me through this?'

I came to myself and began to think, *'How DARE the devil try to take time off of MY LIFE! He did not give me this life! JESUS DID! So how is the devil going to try to get me to choose life or have a child?*

I chose life when I accepted Jesus Christ as my Savior and Christ gives life, including babies.

Well, the devil was only trying to do what he came to do—**"The thief cometh not but for to steal, to kill, and to destroy: I am come that they might have life, and that they might have it more abundantly" (John 10:10).** Jesus said that we *might* have life. The word might, suggests that we can choose to have life and have it abundantly – God gives us free will. God does not force Himself on anyone.

Although I tried to remain calm, that news was a shocker. I went to one of my sisters in Christ who tried to keep me calm by talking to me. "It isn't that bad," she said.

While she was talking to me, God was talking to me too; ***"Be still and know that I am God"*** **(Psalm 46:10).** He said, **"You won't need to have an operation, just stand and have faith in Me—just have faith in Me."**

At first I was trying to decide if I should tell my husband, and if so, when? I decided, of course I will tell him as soon as I can. The devil is a liar and Jesus is Lord. The question remained, how would I tell him? How would I say it? "Help me Lord."

...I changed my clothes and took care of the kids. Our oldest daughter, Tanisha, was living with us at the time. I took a cab to meet Robert at work because I wanted to be there before he got off.

The Holy Spirit had already prepared the way. Robert was glad to see me and asked me if everything was okay. I answered, "Yes, but I just wanted to talk to you," Robert could see that something was on my mind.

STAINED by HIS BLOOD

I waited in our car until he got off work. When he met me in the car, I explained the phone call I had with the doctor and what he said to me.

My husband looked at me and said, "That is the enemy and don't you receive what the doctor said, that is the enemy and don't you believe it either."

Wow! Robert would not even receive, accept or embrace the bad news, not even for a second (Thank you Lord for preparing him). After that discussion, we went out to get something to eat. We sat in the car, and ate, and discussed the situation again, and what we were going to believe. We will stand on God's Word.

STAINED by HIS BLOOD

Before we went home, I asked if we could go down to the church and praise God for our healing although I could praise Him anywhere I was prompted to go to church. So, on our way into the sanctuary there was a class going on and I heard the voice of my roommate, the one with whom I had shared a room on the retreat. She was talking about Jesus and I stuck my head in after she got finish talking.

I asked if we could talk to her, while trying not to draw too much attention to myself, she came out into the sanctuary with us and I told her what the doctor had told me.

She said, "That is what the enemy throws at you when he can't get you any other way. His next step, most of the time is to try to inflict your body with some kind of sickness or disease. He is mad at you because you received something that he did not want you to get (or hear)—FAITH! You got it and you ran with it!" Again, she said, "Faith."

Then she said, "Praise God, let's pray." She began to pray for me and began to lift me up before God.

Robert and I praised God for my healing. We confessed that God is God and that His Word said that, **"with His stripes I am healed"** *(Isaiah 53:5).* The anointing was present, I felt lighter and I felt God's presence as we praised His Name.

After praising the Lord, our sister in Christ told us what to do next. The Holy Spirit was speaking through her. She told Robert as often as he thought about it to anoint my stomach with oil and to pray a healing scripture. She said that I should praise God (without ceasing) for my healing. Robert and I continued to praise and worship God all the way home. That night God had me to anoint my body with oil, and told me I would not have to do this again. I even took a teaspoon by mouth.

NOTES

CHAPTER 10

Whose Report Will You Believe?

Dream

That night, I tossed and turned. I dreamed that I was in a cemetery and there were dead bodies exposed everywhere. There were faces I had never seen before a lot of white faces I am Afro-American, I saw none of my color. I guess the enemy was trying to point out that these people were dead. He was really trying his best to scare me to death.

The enemy was trying hard to steal my faith. I woke up and started to praise God for my healing—"Hallelujah, thank you Lord for healing me." I laid back down repeating 1Peter 2:24, **"By whose stripes ye (I) were healed."** I slept with my Bible under my pillow so that I would have it in case I woke up in the middle of the night. I would have it by me to read.

STAINED by HIS BLOOD

I reminded myself that *'this means I am healed already.'* It also means that Jesus already sees me healed and that the doctor's report have to eventually line up with God's report and what God's Word says about me. I chose to believe God's report. Why not?—wouldn't you?

My belief in God's Word did not stop the enemy from coming at me every chance he could to remind me of what the doctor said about me.

Battle in the Mind

About a week later, the doctor called me back with the specialist number. I called the Cancer Specialist and was told that he was on vacation for the next two weeks. "Okay", I responded, "then put me down the week he comes back" in the meantime Shelia, one of my friends, called me, one who knew what I was diagnosed with. One that God sent to pray with me and I told her that I just made an appointment to see the cancer specialist in two weeks because he was out on vacation for the next two weeks. She said, good I just called to pray with you. She did and hung up. Two weeks passed. I woke up feeling tired since I had not slept much.

After seeing Robert off to work and Tanisha off to school, I fed Ebonee, gave her a bath and played with her for a while.

STAINED by HIS BLOOD

Ebonee and I then went to the grocery store to pick up a few things for dinner. While we were standing in line to check out, here comes the devil, trying to attack my mind with thoughts like, '*shop now because this may be your last time to shop.*' I replied, "Not so, devil!"

When I got home, a sister from the choir called me because she wanted to pray with me. That call was right on time. Robert called during the day, as usual. He wanted to see how my day was going. Of course I told him, "All is well," because it was. I wanted him to work without having to worry about me, especially since I did not know exactly how he was feeling about this whole thing.

STAINED by HIS BLOOD

Confess The Word Boldly and Stand

While the enemy was on duty trying to put fear in us I wanted my husband to hear me speak that his wife is doing well and that I am not going anywhere because I am healed in Jesus name! Did the devil think that I was going to leave my beautiful little girl for someone else to raise or leave my good looking, saved and sanctified husband for someone else to enjoy?—I THINK NOT! I really had something to fight for. The devil is a liar and Jesus is the Messiah.

Take Authority Over The Enemy

...I gave Ebonee her lunch and put her down for her nap. I then sat down in the living room because I needed some sleep. However, there was an eerie feeling that I was not "alone" in my house.

The presence did not feel like the presence of God, even though I knew He was with me. I realized the devil was lurking around. Like I said, I was tired and needed some sleep and I was going to get some. I got up, and told the devil that he is a liar and commanded him, "In the name of Jesus, YOU LEAVE MY HOUSE NOW!" I got the broom and started sweeping.

That's right! I swept him down the stairs and out the front door. I shouted **Get Out!** I did not care who heard me. I went back upstairs, closed my door, sat down and that feeling was gone. There was a peace, so I took a nap and it was a good one. **"I will both lay me down in peace, and sleep: for thou, Lord, only makest me dwell in safety" Psalms 4:8.**

Mind, Kept in Perfect Peace

When I woke up, I was guided by, the Holy Spirit to pray and to read the Word. You see, I had to hear from God every moment. My mind had to be on Him throughout each day. The Holy Spirit did an excellent job in guiding me through each moment of the day.

Now when I say that I had to hear from God, I mean the Holy Spirit made sure that I was not wasting any time focusing on things other than what God said about me.

For instance, when I watched television, it was on the Christian station where someone would be teaching about healing or faith. Even when I turned on the radio, someone was talking about healing. The Holy Spirit guided me into everything I had to do for each day, while waiting for my healing to manifest.

STAINED by HIS BLOOD

Thou wilt keep him in perfect peace, whose mind is stayed on thee: because he trusteth in thee, Isaiah 26:3.

The Holy Spirit helped me to keep up with my housework and made sure that the kids and my husband were taken care of. They never saw me crying or looking sad. In fact, I don't think Tanisha knew what was going on.

Robert and I spoke with our parents often and visited them when we could. Everything had to be running as normal as possible, just as it did before the diagnosis. That was vitally important, The Holy Spirit did not allow us to share with everyone what we were going through. This was very important because we did not want any unbelief or negative spirits calling us just to say, "How are you feeling? What did the doctor say today?" "You know, this or that family member had cancer," or, "I had a friend who had cancer," etc.

However, in spite of our efforts, the enemy still came to remind me of all the family members that died of cancer. I guess he thought that he would really get to me by reminding me of my sister Marsha's death—'Why would God heal you and let all of those other people die? Why should you be any different?' I replied, **"I don't know why they died and maybe I do but the truth is that God is still a healer no matter who died"**.

Be Afraid Devil

You know I *"read"* the devil real good! "First of all, you lying demon, I don't know why they died and even if I did know, what does that have to do with me? What I have learned about my Father God, through spending time with Him daily(reading His Word) and hearing about Him through men of God, is that God does not kill people.

He came that we might have life and have it more abundantly. You, the enemy, came to kill, to steal and to destroy.

You! killed them early. You took their lives from them.

Well, because I know what I know now I'm going to tell the truth, you are the killer, not Jesus!" "Because I know what I know now, the doctor's report will line up with the Word of God and with what the Word said about me.

'By Jesus' stripes I was already healed' and I am going to tell it. I am going to tell about all the tricks you tried to pull on me and I am not going to wait for the doctor's report to receive what my Heavenly Father has already given me.

I believe God's report right now! I know God has healed me. I stand in faith, my faith is going to bring to past the manifestation of my healing, and that is what you are afraid of. So, <u>be afraid devil</u> because healing is mine!"

STAINED by HIS BLOOD

After that, I went to the Father and poured out my heart and said, "Lord, I know who died of what in my family and among friends but, I am not here for them. They are gone and this is for others and me. You said you are a healer and that if I stand on your Word, in faith, and not doubt in my heart, that my healing will come to me. Healing come to me now, in the name of Jesus!

The doctor's reports have to say what your report says about me Lord. Until it does, I will keep confessing and I will keep fighting the good fight of faith using *1Peter 2:24 "Who his own self bare our sins in his own body on the tree that we being dead to sins, should live unto righteousness: by whose stripes ye (I am) were healed"*. **Like a great man of God said "*I am the healed protecting my health*".**

STAINED by HIS BLOOD

I already have the victory! I believe God! Not looking to the left or to the right. I prepared for war by putting on the Spiritual Armour of God.

Finally, my brethren, be strong in the Lord, and in the power of his might. Put on the whole armor of God, that ye may be able to stand against the wiles of the devil. For we wrestle not against flesh and blood. But against principalities, against powers, against the ruler of darkness of this world, against spiritual wickedness in high places. Wherefore take unto you the whole armour of God, that ye may be able to withstand in the evil day, and having done all, to stand.

STAINED by HIS BLOOD

Stand therefore, having your loins girt about with truth, and having on the breastplate of righteousness; And your feet shod with the preparation of the gospel of peace; Above all, taking the shield of faith wherewith ye shall be able to quench all the fiery darts of the wicked.

And take the helmet of salvation, and the sword of the Spirit, which is the word of God: Praying always with all prayer and supplication in the Spirit, and watching thereunto with all perseverance and supplication for all saints; Ephesians 6:10-18

NOTES

CHAPTER 11

Speak The Word Only

Each day my faith was challenged. I had to read the Word or listen to it on tape, television or radio. Sometimes I had to sing myself happy.

During my wait to see the cancer specialist I had grown so much in faith that I knew when I had my doctor's visit (no matter what other tests I had to take) I was already healed. It did not matter what negative report came up—I was healed! I had no fear in saying the word "cancer" and it did not scare me to say it anymore because I had God's Word—I know who I am in Christ.

My son, ATTEND TO MY WORDS; incline thine ear unto my sayings. Let them not depart from thine eyes; keep them in the midst of thine heart. For they are life unto those that find them, and health to all their flesh (Proverbs 4:20-22).

Every knee must bow at the name of Jesus and every tongue must confess that He is Lord (Romans 14:11) and that included cancer and any other sickness, disease and pain. Hallelujah, Glory to God! I KNEW that cancer had to bow down to me, in the name of Jesus, because **1John 4:4 says Ye are of God, little children, and have overcome them: because greater is he that is in you, than he that is in the world.**

Oh boy!—the enemy was in trouble! I got power over *him*! I got authority over *him*...because the Greater One, Jesus, lives big in *me*! I had fed myself with so much of God's Word that the enemy could not stand it. He tried his best to make me confess that I had cancer but I would NEVER give in.

STAINED by HIS BLOOD

I did not have cancer because Jesus took it on his body to the cross. With as many stripes as Jesus bore on that cross, I know cancer was one of them! Listen, even though the doctors, diagnosed me with ovarian cancer, I went to my Father God and in His Word He said that He came that I may have life,

John 10:10 says, The thief cometh not, but for to steal, and to kill and to destroy: I am come that they might have lift, and that they might have it and that they might have it more abundantly. The Word of God says **Let God be true, but every man a liar (Romans 3:4).** Please don't get me wrong, I'm not saying doctors are bad, because they are not… they are there to help us.

I believe that God put doctors in place to help us. The doctors give diagnoses and medicine for the physical body to feel and get better.

STAINED by HIS BLOOD

When we get evil reports of sickness and diseases that's going to take our life against our will, I disagree that their report is final, and that it is only final, if it's received or accepted by that individual.

What do you believe? I believe Christians have a choice to be healed and live here on earth longer to fulfill the kingdom of God to complete the will of God or go home to be with our heavenly father. Going home to be with our father is not a bad thing but, why let sickness or disease make that decision for us when we have the authority to choose to believe God's report and the power of God to be healed.

Ovarian cancer did not line up with what my Father said. That evil report was straight from the devil so I decided not to receive it, my choice. In fact, I gave it back to him!

My Father said cancer is not mine so why would I want something that God did not give me; something that would hurt me, take my life or send me home early without completing my assignment down here on earth?

God promised this—**With long life will I satisfy him, and show him my salvation (Psalm 91:16).** I was not ready to go to heaven yet; I knew that His will was not completed in me or for me. I still had a husband to tend to and children to raise; as well as souls to witness to about our Lord and Savior Jesus Christ.

If I did not want to be sick and was not ready to go 'home' then **I had to fight the good fight of faith (I Timothy 6:12).** I had a choice to both be in faith and live, or to take on fear and go home.

I decided to fight the good fight of faith with the Word of God and receive the healing that God had already given to me.

STAINED by HIS BLOOD

This was, AND IS, the will of the Father; it is in His Word, it is His will! For me to live and not die! It's my blood bought right to be healed.

Well, the enemy decided to pay me a visit through another dream (again). There was a play going on in this huge auditorium, and the place was packed, not an empty seat in the house. I walked on the stage and asked, "What is the name of the play?" I wanted to know the name because there were so many people present – I figured it had to be a good play. The auditorium became quiet and suddenly (on one accord) the whole audience yelled, **"Snow White and the Seven Dwarfs."** To this day, I do not know why that particular story was chosen. I guess it was because Snow White dies in the story.

However, she gets up and lives. I don't know why this play was chosen. Then I asked, "Who is playing Snow White?"—you know we always want to know whose playing the lead character.

The audience shouted again, in unison, **"You are!"** And in unison they began to shout, *"**Read! Read the script!**"* repeatedly while someone was handing me the script. Now isn't that just like the devil! He can't do a thing by himself.

In the natural realm, they thought they were just whipping Jesus but in the spirit realm, the devil was being whipped and stripped. Jesus stripped him of his powers, and gave them to us. Colossians 2:15 in The Amplified says, **[God] disarmed the principalities and powers that were ranged against us and made a bold display and public example of them, in triumphing over them in Him and in it [the cross].** The King James Version says**, And having spoiled principalities and powers, he made a shew of them openly, triumphing over them in it.**

STAINED by HIS BLOOD

I have the power to live, and not die. I have the power to walk in love, prosperity, and integrity, and forgiveness etc. I have no more shame, low self-esteem, guiltiness, embarrassment, no lack of any kind in my life. I have a boldness that makes my Father God proud to call me His daughter. How could I not walk with my head up and speak with such authority with God as my Father and Jesus as my brother what do I (we) have to be afraid of?

I looked at the script, as the audience grew silent; you could have heard a pin drop. I looked over the script and read it with my eyes. I saw only a few words in bold lettering which read, *'I HAVE OVARIAN CANCER.'* As I hesitated to read it aloud, the audience shouted again in unison, *"**Read it! Read It!**"*...and then they got *very* quiet.

STAINED by HIS BLOOD

This time I got angry because I knew who had written those words! I felt his presence sitting behind me so I turned around slowly, dropping the paper on the floor. I tell you the truth, if I thought a good physical fist fight would have beaten him, I would have did it and won.

The Bible tells me, *For we wrestle not against flesh and blood, but against principalities, against powers, against the rulers of the darkness of this world, against spiritual wickedness in high places, Ephesians 6:12.* Therefore, I did not attempt to fight the devil in the physical realm.

I knew the Word of God would hit him where it hurts so I began to speak Isaiah 53:5 from my heart—*But he was wounded for my transgressions, He was bruised for my iniquities: the chastisement of my peace was upon him; and with His stripes I am healed!*

STAINED by HIS BLOOD

Immediately, I went into another dream where I was sitting in this beautiful garden on a white bench where there were plants and trees that were so green all around me. There was a fountain with running water, a waterfall and more plants and trees behind me and I could hear birds singing; I do not believe there is a garden like this, anywhere on this earth that I could go see.

As I was sitting in the garden (topless), milk began to flow out of my breasts (life more abundantly).

It was a calm and pleasant atmosphere. It was so peaceful, and the aroma was clean and fresh...I felt the presence of God there.

Although I was sitting alone, I was not alone, He was there, God was there! He was all around; He was in the air, He was on the plants and in the clear water. The water was clean and it looked so soft.

STAINED by HIS BLOOD

I could hear Him through the birds as they sang, and I could see Him flying through the beautiful butterflies. I was not bitten once by a bug, although I was surrounded by all the water and all types of plants. He was in the color of the flowers and in the green plants. I had never seen plants this color green before....

In my third week, I called the Cancer Specialist back to confirm my appointment to come in for the following day. I called also, to make sure he was back from his vacation. "Hi this is Mareen Oliver and I am calling to confirm my appointment for tomorrow morning at 10am". The registration staff said, *"what is your name again"*? "Mareen Oliver" *"I'm sorry mam I have no confirm appointment for you on tomorrow morning".*

STAINED by HIS BLOOD

I said I made the appointment 2 weeks ago because the doctor was on vacation for 2 weeks and had already been on vacation for 1 week when I called to make the appointment so; he was out the office for a total of 3 weeks right? She replied, *"Yes that is correct, but Mrs. Oliver I am checking the whole week and I do not see your name at all and I am the one who take the calls for appointments, and I don't remember making the appointment for you.*

I can schedule one for you now it would be in the next weeks". I said "ok" but I am sure that I made the appointment for this Tuesday at 10a.m. I asked her "Are you sure you don't see my name anywhere what about next week? *"No mam" I am even looking in the rest of this month and next month and we do not have an appointment scheduled for you.* I am puzzled now, because I know I called and scheduled an appointment. I hung up and called Shelia because I remember talking to her right after I made the appointment.

STAINED by HIS BLOOD

Shelia, do you remember 2 weeks ago when I made an appointment to see the Cancer Specialist I asked? She replied, *"yes you told me you had just got off the phone with the office and that the doctor was on vacation and didn't you schedule it for tomorrow?"* Yes, I did, well; they told me they do not have me scheduled at all this week, next week, nor next month. I do not understand this; I guess it just gives me more time to build my faith, huh? *"Yep"*, okay, thank you, *"you are welcome bye"*, bye.

STAINED by HIS BLOOD

NOTES

CHAPTER 12

Persecution Prayer and Praise

STAINED by HIS BLOOD

Five weeks had gone bye, I made an appointment to go and see my doctor again. I knew God had healed me. I did not care what the test reported or what the doctors reported. I wanted him to take another ultra sound to confirm what I already knew—I did NOT need to see a Cancer Specialist next week. While I was waiting inside of the doctor's office, I kept God's Word before me as I had from the beginning of this whole journey. Finally, my name was called and as Ebonee and I walked into the examination room, I noticed that it was not my doctor sitting there, but it was his partner. I had seen him before when I had my ovary removed. He came to see me during my doctors off day.

Even though they worked together, he was not the one I wanted to see that day. He explained to me that it was my doctor's off day. I wondered why no one told me this when I made the appointment, I would have rescheduled.

STAINED by HIS BLOOD

I sat and watched as he looked over my report and when he looked up, I asked him if he remembered me.

He said, *"How could I forget a beautiful black young lady like you."* **I am not here for your compliments; I am here to take care of business,** these were my thoughts.

"Mrs. Oliver, as I look at your report, you were supposed to see a cancer specialist long before now." "Yes, I know but when I called to make an appointment I was told that that the Cancer Specialist was on vacation and would not be available for the next two weeks". "I called to confirm my appointment and I was told that I did not have one and I scheduled to see him next week. I am here today because; I would like to be re-tested, for another ultrasound, to get my good news. I know that God has healed me."

STAINED by HIS BLOOD

The doctor just ignored me and told me *"you did not try to see the doctor"*. Was he calling me a liar? *"You need to see a doctor as soon as possible."*

The doctor continued ignoring everything I said and anything I attempted to say, I think he just did not understand and was scared for me. He turned to my daughter and said to her, "Your hair is so pretty; who did your hair?"

Ebonee replied, "Mommy." "Who dressed you?" "Mommy."

I thought to myself, my daughter did not come to see you. Does he know that her name is not Mrs. Oliver? *"You need your mommy don't you...you help mommy and make sure she keeps her doctor's appointment."* Ebonee's facial expression said it all, "What is he talking about?" He went on to say, *"Matter of fact, I am going to make an appointment for her right now."*

He dialed and asked the person on the other end *"What days and times do you have available for her to see the Cancer Specialist, I need an appointment for her immediately,"* that person put him on hold. Therefore, while he was waiting, I attempted to tell him that God healed me and that I just needed to take another ultrasound to confirm it.

Again, the doctor ignored everything I said and continued to talk to the registration person, *"As soon as possible."* Then, he finally decided he wanted to talk to me and asked, *"Can you see the doctor on this evening Mrs. Oliver?"* "Where is he located?" *"He is in his Oak Brook office."* "No, that's too far, I am not driving today." *"I will pay for your cab fare there and back."*

Well, the Holy Spirit reminded me that, that night was Bible class and that I needed to be there so, I said, "No, I can't go today, I have Bible class."

STAINED by HIS BLOOD

The doctor looked worried while he made the appointment for that following Monday at the hospital. He had a look of complete disbelief regarding my decision to postpone seeing the Cancer Specialist that night. After he got off the phone, I attempted to tell him again, "You are not listening to me; I told you that God healed me".

Just let me take the test over and if it still shows a negative report then I will go ahead with my appointment."—he would not hear me.

He shouted, Well, I thought this was funny, Him shouting at me because of something I did not want to do. *"No! Mrs. Oliver, I am not listening to you! I don't care what you got set up in your pretty little head or what your beliefs are. You need to see the doctor as soon as possible!"* I told you he was scared for me, he meant well.

Then he turned to Ebonee, I am thinking here he goes again talking to my two year old as if I was dying, *"Who combed your hair this morning, it is so pretty?"* I thought, *'What's up with him asking her that question again...maybe he's the one that needs to see a doctor for a memory check.'* "You need your mommy don't you?" "Yes," Ebonee replied. *"Make sure mommy keeps her appointment."* Why would I not keep the appointment?—I had no fear I thought to myself.

As we stood waiting for the bus to go home, a spirit of depression came around. I rebuked it. The enemy wanted me to think on the things that the doctor said to me but I didn't and I wouldn't! Romans 3:4a says, **God forbid: yea, let God be true, but every man a liar.** If I say that I am not healed then I am a liar because His Word says that I am and He cannot lie. The enemy wanted to break my faith down and wanted me to let go of what my Father said about me.

STAINED by HIS BLOOD

NO WAY UNDER NO CIRCUMSTANCES—*by Jesus' stripes I am healed!*

That night, I went to Bible class and received some more teaching on faith. My faith increased every time I went to class. I thanked God for my Bible class teacher Mrs. Carrell for allowing God to use her to teach on the Word on Faith during my time of need although she did not know I needed it but, God did.

Our church was going through some changes and I could not get what I needed in Sunday morning service. I would go to church on Sunday and come back home the same way I went. Sometimes I wondered why I bothered going.

It is so important to go to a church that teaches God's Word. Each time I attended Bible class I received a revelation on faith and healing. I took that revelation and meditated on it all week.

STAINED by HIS BLOOD

The Word strengthened me; and because I had the Word in my heart, I sang praises to God even more. I had a tight relationship with God and I wanted to pray and talk to Him daily. The routine became a part of me. You know, he actually talks back to you. I began to love Him more and I knew without a doubt that He loved me and would not lie to me. **He is who He says he is; He is King of kings and Lord of lords; He is the Great I Am; and I was really getting to know Him as a Healer—WOW!**

The Sunday before my doctor's appointment, I praised God like never before. I had "eaten" so much of the Word that I was running over with praise and joy—*I will bless the Lord at all times: his praise shall continually be in my mouth* **(Psalm 34:1).** "Hallelujah" kept coming out of my mouth. I danced in the Holy Spirit until the anointing was upon me so strong that I was spiritually drunk, I could not stand up straight.

STAINED by HIS BLOOD

My roommate from the Women's Retreat took me out of the choir stand and into an enclosed room, which was adjacent to the choir stand.

She left me alone so that I could praise God without disturbing what was going on in the service. I continued to praise God; I was NOT going to let Him go! I just wanted to stay in His presence, it was so peaceful there.

My roommate came back about fifteen minutes later and wiped the tears as they were flowing from down my face. Then she started dusting me off and asked how my skirt got so dirty? I wanted to tell her that I had been on the floor before God and that I did not care what I had on but I was still in the Spirit and I chose not to speak to her right then I was not ready to let God go.

I kept my doctor's appointment with the cancer specialist. Sharon took me and, stayed with me.

STAINED by HIS BLOOD

She sat on the other side of the curtain during my examination. The doctor asked me many questions, such as, *"Have you ever been hospitalized?—When?—Why?"* My roommate then asked *him* questions from the other side of the curtains. "Doctor, are you saved? ...do you believe in healing? ...and what are your beliefs?" He said, *"My beliefs are Allah, I am Muslim."* I am so glad that I was not going by what he believed.

Sharon kept talking with the Cancer Specialist "You see, I and that Christian woman that you have over there on that table believe in the Father, His Son, Jesus Christ, and the Holy Spirit. We believe in ***Isaiah 53:1, Who hath believed our report? And to whom is the arm of the Lord revealed.***"

The doctor asked Sharon was she my sister. Sharon replied yes.

STAINED by HIS BLOOD

He just kept on examining me. "Ouch!" I said, as he pressed upon my stomach right below my naval. *"Do you feel pain right there?"* he asked. "Yes, I had surgery two and a half years ago when I had a cesarean and also a year ago when my left ovary was removed." Sharon hollered out from on the other side of the curtain to me "That's why you are in pain, you are not fully healed yet, it takes time and I have had the same surgery years ago". The doctor responded by saying, "*I see it runs in your family* (we are not even related like that, he was guessing).

As the doctor completed his exam with me, he scheduled an appointment for me to have more tests done on the following day.

Later that night I tossed and turned. At about 1 a.m. the phone rang and it was a dear sister, who was crying, and going through some marital problems.

She needed me to listen and to pray with her. She did not know what I was going through, and I was not led to tell her because, this particular phone call was not about me, it was about her.

The Holy Spirit led me to listen to her and to give her words of encouragement with what God had said about her situation. I ended the call with a prayer; she felt better and so did I. Even though I did feel better, it would not have mattered how I felt, good or bad, that time was about her. I did not wish what I was going through on anyone.

You know, when you sing or say the words, "Lord, use me to help someone, use me to bless someone," you should mean those words; because you do not know when He is going to use you. The time of day, and what is going on in your life, at that moment, does not matter to God when He chooses to use you. You just have to trust Him and obey Him. He will take care of you and all of your needs and desires.

STAINED by HIS BLOOD

Your faith will be tested time after time in this faith walk. It does not have to be in sickness or in diseases but whatever the case, you should believe what you say when you say it. Have faith in what you confess about, when you speak The Word of God.

NOTES

CHAPTER 13

All Is Well

STAINED by HIS BLOOD

Robert went with me to my appointment the next morning. I had to take several tests Blood, CAT scan, Heart, and Chest X-ray.

I was called into the area where they took samples of blood. As I sat down, I noticed there were six or seven long empty tubes and I asked the nurse if all of those tubes were for me. *"What do you think?"* she replied. *"You are the only one here."*

You know I did not need her sarcasm. I replied, "I don't know...they could have been sitting there for you to use as needed, and if you are not having a good morning then keep it to yourself or tell Jesus about it. Maybe this is not the career for you." I'm thinking to myself, she did not know why I or perhaps anyone had to come to this area of the hospital. She did not know how people were feeling or maybe it just did not matter because of what she was going through.

Maybe she did not know how to take it to God or know how to get over whatever was troubling her. I prayed, "God, forgive me, and help her."

While she filled those tubes with my blood, I repeated **Isaiah 53:5—and with his stripes I am healed.** Okay, I finished that test and went on to the next one in another room because I had to have a test performed on my heart. While the nurse placed these little black things (called bulbs) all over my chest, I repeated Isaiah 53:5—"Thank you Lord for healing me!" I finished that test and went on to the next one, which was a CT scan (CAT scan). What a name, "cat scan"—it sounds as though someone is going to skin a cat!

Before I took the test, a nurse brought me a cup filled with a white liquid and instructed me to drink all of it because she had two more of those cups for me to drink. She said it would help the doctor to see my organs better when taking the CAT scan.

While I was drinking, I remembered a prayer a sister name Kimmley had prayed for me the night before; she prayed that I would count it *all* joy.

James 1:2, 3 says, My brethren, count it all joy when ye fall into divers temptations; Knowing *this,* that the trying of your faith worketh patience. I wondered, *'Where is the joy and when is it going to come?'* As I forced myself to drink, I spoke these words to my father God. *"I know that by your stripes I am healed so why don't you stop this now? Why do I have to go through all of these tests?"* At that particular point in time, I was probably just tired of going through the motions, or was I losing something here? *'Calm down Mareen, as I said to myself.*

With this in mind, I calmed down, knowing that I was going to come through this with a positive report.

STAINED by HIS BLOOD

After drinking all three cups, I took out my Bible and started to read a number of scriptures. Robert looked up from his newspaper at me and said, "It's going to be alright." About thirty minutes later, the doctor came in.

He took me into a room so that I could change into one of those hospital gowns and helped me onto a table and strapped my arms and legs down.

I felt like I was going to the 'loony bin' or was trying to escape from one. *No, just kidding.*

The table started moving into a machine that was shaped like a tunnel or even a casket— *'couldn't they have come up with a better looking device than this one!'* I thought. *"...I am not dead devil; I don't care what it looks like."* It was cold and eerie inside of the machine. I was instructed to hold my breath each time an x-ray was taken while strapped in the tunnel. This went on for about fifteen to twenty minutes.

Just when I thought that test was over, the nurses took me out of the contraption, inserted an I.V. into my arm and then pushed me back into the same machine. **"By his stripes I am heale**d—Lord get me out of here!" I repeated to myself.

I finished that test "woo hoo!" there was one more to go. Next was the chest x-ray. My routine for that day was clothes on—clothes off. While I was waiting patiently to be called, my sister Spring came in. She said she wanted to be there with us. I thought that was nice of her to take time out to come sit with us.

Then she apologized for not being there earlier. We were glad she came anyway. ...I continued repeating Isaiah 53:5. God took me through all the tests, it was a workout but I was finished until the following week. I had one more test to take and then the good report would be on paper! This is what I believed.

STAINED by HIS BLOOD

That night I went to bed early (about 8 p.m.) This was funny; I used to be a night owl. At around 10:30 p.m. my pastor's daughter Donna called me. *"Mo, are you alright? One of the church mothers and I were wondering where you were. We missed you this past Sunday and we wanted to know if you were alright?"* "Oh, yes. I stayed in to rest and did some meditating because I knew that I had to have some tests done but I am okay, and thank you for calling." *"Okay, sorry to wake you, go back to sleep."* "Okay I replied."

The enemy came soon after I hung up the phone and he said, *"You must be getting really sick because you are just so tired and weak. You don't go to bed this early."* And because I was tired, my mind started to think, "Yes, I am tired—Oh NO!!!" I started dialing one of the sisters' phone numbers, "Shelia gave me a scripture". **Do you see what the enemy does when you are tired? He starts to work on you.**

STAINED by HIS BLOOD

He really takes advantage of you when he thinks that you are at your weakest point. She gave me a scripture and I hung up. Then I immediately grabbed my Bible and read the scripture she had given me. I fell back to sleep (again) with my face in my Bible. I woke up again hearing those same words, *"You must be getting really sick, you are so weak."* I got up and sat in the living room with my husband.

He was turning off the television to come to bed and I asked him "where are you going?" He said to bed and asked me if I knew what time, it was. He then told me it was 12:30 a.m. I said, "Oh really," and I continued to stay up.

Well, it's no surprise that the enemy came again and said, *"You know they only took x-rays of the right side of your chest. They MUST have seen SOMETHING...AND you are SOOO tired,"* 'Yes, they did,' I thought to myself.

Right then the Holy Spirit spoke to me and said, "Mareen you are *supposed* to be tired. You took several different tests today and for one of them, you gave many tubes of blood—you are *supposed* to be tired. Go to bed my child." The rest of the night, I slept peacefully in God's arms like a newborn baby.

The following week I went to take the final test. "A vaginal ultrasound". The physician that accompanied the Cancer Specialist during my first testing also conducted this last test. While I was waiting to be called, I felt something was missing, I felt as though I had forgotten something. I DID!—I forgot my Bible! *'Now what am I going to do?'* I thought to myself. I needed to read (or hear) the Word of God, I needed to know that everything was still alright (and why wouldn't it be). Having the Word of God gave me that much needed inner peace.

STAINED by HIS BLOOD

Although I had been in my Word day and night as stated in, **Joshua 1:8a This book of the law shall not depart out of thy mouth; but thou shalt meditate therein day and night.**

It did not stop the enemy from coming with some kind of discouraging words to make me feel uncomfortable about what I was standing on(this is one of the things he does for a living).

I remember the parable about The Sower Soweth the Word in Mark 4:14-20 it says,

And these are they by the way side, where the word is sown; but when they have heard, Satan cometh immediately, and taketh away the word that was sown into their hearts.

STAINED by HIS BLOOD

And these are they likewise which are sown on stony ground; who, when they have heard the word, immediately receive it with gladness;

And have no root in themselves, and so endure but for a time; afterward, when affliction or persecution ariseth for the word's sake, immediately they are offended.

And these are they which are sown among thorns; such as hear the word,

And the cares of this world, and the deceitfulness of riches, and the lusts of other things entering in, choke the word, and it becometh unfruitful.

And these are they which are sown on good ground; such as hear the word, and receive it, and bring forth fruit , some thirtyfold, some sixty fold and some an hundred.

STAINED by HIS BLOOD

The Holy Spirit then brought a scripture to my remembrance and I quoted it. Another one came, and then another one, and then more. Wow! I had no idea that I knew that many scriptures. They started to flow out of my mouth. Now, I did not know exactly what book or chapter most of them came from but I knew they were in the Bible. I had read these scriptures several times. I guess you can say "they were hidden in my heart for a time such as this!" and I promised to keep them there always. No matter what comes, I have Jesus with me always—**For he hath said, I will never leave thee nor forsake thee** in **Hebrews 13:5b. Thank you Holy Spirit!**

STAINED by HIS BLOOD

Finally, I was called into the examination room. While the doctor examined me, he asked me a series of questions. While he was asking me questions, you know what I was doing? I was confessing within myself, "By Jesus' stripes I am healed—Lord, get me out of here." As the doctor looked at the monitor and continued his examination, he asked, *"Mrs. Oliver, you said that you had an ovary removed some time ago?"* "We went over this last week...didn't he write it down...that should have been on my chart...why didn't he look at my chart...." I thought. "Yes," I replied. *"Which ovary was removed?"* he asked.

'Oh boy, does he know what he is doing...isn't he looking at the monitor?' "My left ovary was removed," I replied. *"Oh, it didn't look like it,"* he explained. *"And why was it removed?"*

STAINED by HIS BLOOD

"Because of a fibroid tumor," I explained. He said, *"That is what these look like."* Thank you Lord. *"Okay Mrs. Oliver, you may get dressed and go, and I will see you tomorrow with all of your test results."* I went home, praising God for the victory!

STAINED by HIS BLOOD

NOTES

CHAPTER 14

None Of The Above!

STAINED by HIS BLOOD

The evening before I received my test results, I had a talk with Robert. I said:

"I don't know if the test results are going to line up with God's report at this time but I do know that eventually they will. When?..... I do not know but I know they will. No matter what else I may have to go through, no matter what pain I might feel, I know that **by His stripes I am healed**. I might leave from here on earth, but if I do, I will still declare that God is a Healer and that I am still Healed, even then, I believe that God, my Father, would bring me back or send someone to raise me up. The enemy will not have my faith!—no matter what happens.

He cannot make me see it any other way. God Is a Healer, no matter what happens, I trust HIM all the way to the end of this!

Immediately after speaking those words, I felt a release, a peace and a comfort.

STAINED by HIS BLOOD

I heard the enemy say these words in the spirit *"I give up, I can't do anything else, She's going to believe God's Word till the end"*. That was not to say that he would not continue to try to steal my faith, I still did not trust him and I will never trust the enemy! He never changes; he will always be a liar, and a deceiver etc. I was determined to trust God and declare that He is a Healer and I was healed no matter what the outcome. So the following morning I received a phone call from a co-worker Ethel, *"Mareen, don't you have to go to the doctor today?"* *"Yes, I do."* *"Is Robert going with you?"* *"No, he has to work."* *"Well, I am not going to let you go by yourself, I am going with you. What time do you have to be there?* *"10 a.m."* *"I will meet you there, goodbye."*

She hung up before I could convince her that she did not have to come, especially since she had to ride the bus as well.

STAINED by HIS BLOOD

Every one of the Sisters in Christ that I have mentioned, God had placed in my life for a season to pray for me and to encourage me. Robert and I did not go through this alone. While the sisters were praying for me, it was important that I maintained faith that God had healed me. It was my decision to accept healing through Jesus Christ **Mark 11:24 says, Therefore I say unto you, What things soever ye desire, when ye pray, believe that ye receive them, and ye shall have them.** A person can pray for someone until they feel tired, but it is up to the person that has been attacked with the condition to believe that God has already healed them.

STAINED by HIS BLOOD

If the person does not want to hold on because of the pain or the difficulty of having their faith tested and is just ready to go home to heaven, then our prayers will have little effect. In my situation, their prayers helped me but *my* faith had to endure—I believed God's Word. Those times when I felt weak and needed some help, their prayers helped me to endure.

While getting dressed, I thanked and praised God for the victory just as I had done over the past few months. It was already done! God's report said that I was healed—**But he was wounded for [Mareen's] transgressions, he was bruised for [Mareen's] iniquities: the chastisement of [Mareen's] peace was upon him and with his stripes [Mareen is] healed, Isaiah 53:5**. Now, I was ready to go and hear the confirmation from man's report.

STAINED by HIS BLOOD

I arrived on time, only to find that the doctors were late. While Ethel and I waited, time passed by quickly as we talked about the goodness of God. Finally, the moment had come. I found myself in a private room with my friend and three doctors.

I said within myself, "With his stripes I am healed, thank you Lord!" The cancer specialist spoke first.

"All of your tests have come back negative." "Hallelujah, thank you Jesus," I said within myself. I sat and looked into the doctor's eyes with no surprise and no shock.

I maintained my composure, having a straight facial expression because I knew what my Father had said in His Word; I had meditated on it, spoke it, prayed about it, praised and thanked Him, and had shouted in victory throughout my healing process. The only thing that the doctor was telling me was that their report had lined up with God's report—it was just confirmation.

By that time, God's Word was so real to me that even if the doctor's report indicated that the tests came back positive, I would have stood even longer on God's Word until the doctor's report lined up with what my father's report said about me.

The doctor spoke again, *"Since we are not sure that the cancer has not hidden somewhere else in your body, we need to do one of the four things."* He looked at me and waited for me to respond, so I did.

"What are the four things that you think you want to do since you are not one hundred percent sure that the cancer is not hidden somewhere else in my body?" *'I've got to hear this,'* I thought to myself. He said, *"Well, the one thing that we could do is give you chemotherapy."*

STAINED by HIS BLOOD

I said, "You want to give me the chemotherapy so that you can be one hundred percent sure. My hair might fall out or my complexion might change from dark to darker from the chemicals that you would inject into my body—*have you lost your the mind*! I could get sick and weak from it, and to top it all off my family could and they would start worrying about something that is nothing."

I asked, "What is number two?" *"Overall surgery,"* he replied. "Now what does that mean?" *"This means we would have to cut your stomach open, down the middle, to take tissues from the lymph nodes to examine, because cancer cells could easily hide there."*

All I could think was, *'thank you Lord for healing me.'* You know, I could see if the tests came back positive, then I would decide what my next step would have been, while waiting for their report to line up with the Word of God but this was not the case.

STAINED by HIS BLOOD

"You want me to check into the hospital so, that you can cut my stomach down the middle so, that I could have a scar there for life (and let's not talk about the hospital bill). You want to do all of this because you are not one hundred percent sure that there are not cancer cells in my body – even though the tests came back negative...NEXT!"

He sighed, and turned and looked at the other two doctors that were in the room and then turned back to me and said, *"We can make an incision by your naval, and take tissues from there."* "You want to cut me there? I have been cut there before, that is another bill and another scar. What's number four?" *"Well, you can come back every two to three months to be examined for cancer,"* he explained. "For how long," I asked. *"For at least 5 years."* There was silence in the room for about thirty seconds or more.

The doctors were looking at me, waiting for me to respond. I was listening to the Holy Spirit without fear of what was presented to me.

STAINED by HIS BLOOD

Then the doctor broke the silence, *"Which one would you like to do?"* As my spiritual father Pastor Bill Winston would say, "Isn't that just like the devil to create a problem where there is no problem and then try to give you a solution to solve it!"

After the Holy Spirit finished explaining to me what to say, I looked at the doctor straight in his eyes and replied, "None—none of the above. But, I will be getting a yearly check-up, as usual." The room fell silent again....

The doctors acted as if they could not hear me clearly or correctly, so I repeated my answer, "I said none, none of the above. I continued to tell him, "I told my doctor's partner that I was **healed**". He did not believe me so; I went along with the steps. I took all of your tests, and they all came back negative and you cannot find anything.

STAINED by HIS BLOOD

Just because you are still not one hundred percent sure, you want to do more testing. Well, I am one hundred percent sure, because the God that I serve has healed me and He cannot lie! I believe His report."

There was complete silence again, but that was okay, this was <u>Great!</u> <u>I had the devil lost for words, striped down butt naked; false teeth fell out of his mouth</u> (Jesus knocked the first set out at the cross). I have the floor I have the authority to say what I am not going to do or take anymore. I know who I am in Christ!

Suddenly, one of the cancer specialist's assistants came up to me. She was a beautiful, slim African American woman. I guess she felt compelled to talk to me. Maybe she thought that I would respond to her differently because I am African American or perhaps because I was a woman as well.

STAINED by HIS BLOOD

I Am A Christian First! She spoke to me in a low tone as if I was a seven year old that she was trying to give a shot to. *"Now Mrs. Oliver, I know that we are probably scaring you..."* Devil, you wish! As I said within myself. *"...but ovarian cancer is nothing to play with. It is one of the top killers of women. It kills fast, so please think about it."*

"You are not scaring me," I said. The cancer specialist walked back over to me, *"Okay, you think about it and call me tomorrow."* I thought, *'What part of **NONE OF THE ABOVE** did they not understand?'* You know the enemy is very persistent and that is the way we should be when we are fighting for what is ours! *We* seem to give up too easily but we must remember what 1Timothy 6:12 says, **"fight the good fight of faith, lay hold on eternal life, whereunto thou art also called, and hast professed a good profession before many witnesses**.

STAINED by HIS BLOOD

NOTES

CHAPTER 15

The Beginning

The Holy Spirits Responds

I replied again **NONE OF THE ABOVE.** I will do my yearly physical as I always do. The head doctor replied" Then I'm going to have to put down that you refused any treatment" *That is fine.* I looked over at my friend and said, "Let's go" we both walked out of the door with smiles. As we were walking to the bus stop she asked me why I did not want to take option four and come back as many times as they wanted me to for check-ups.

I explained to her, *"The Holy Spirit said No,* because if I had agreed to come back as often as they would have wanted me to, somewhere in between those appointments doubt or fear would have attempted to sneak back into my thinking. During each visit to the doctor's I probably would have thought, "Will they find something this time?" This would be living in bondage to the enemy and it is a trap to keep my mind focused on what might show up in those tests.

I do not have time for that. It would be wasting my time and I have too much ministry work to do in the Kingdom of God before Jesus comes back!"

We know that whatever you meditate on becomes your most dominant thought and it would have eaten away at my faith, right down to nothing; then they would have found something because of doubt. The enemy knows that I know he is a liar so he would have made it very hard for me to get my faith back. He would have not only put sickness on me but would have made the pain so unbearable that I would have bowed down to that sickness and pain (because of a lack of faith) and given up and died.

No one can tell my testimony better than I can—how could I do that if I were dead! The devil does not have power over me, and I am not going to ever let him have what Jesus took back on the cross for me.

STAINED by HIS BLOOD

God gave it to me! If I was dead, I would not be a threat to him any longer and no one would get the victory out of that besides him.

Why give him that much power? Why give him time at all when the Word is final—I AM healed. I AM who my Father says that I am and I can do what He says I can do. Most of all, right now I have what He said is mine—healing. Healing is mine! Divine health is mine! I am going to tell this testimony from now on. Besides, what I went through was never about me or for me, but it was to help someone else overcome any doubt that they might have had about our Father God. I was born for a purpose and for such a time as this; to bring souls into the Kingdom of God and lead others back to **Him, John 12:32 says, And I, If I be lifted up from the earth, will draw all *men* unto me.**

I am going to tell what a liar and a deceiver the devil is.

STAINED by HIS BLOOD

I will share all of the tricks he threw at me during this trial. The enemy lost and it is too late now because, what I found out, and now know about my God, and who I am in Christ Jesus, is life to me thank you Lord for **1John 4:4** *Greater is He that is in me than he that is in the world.* My friend and I hugged and rejoiced. I told her how happy I was that she had come and sincerely thanked her for her prayers and for standing in agreement with Robert and I.

She said she would not have had it any other way, and that she was blessed by the whole visit and how our Father God had showed Himself strong through me.

...by this time, our buses were coming so we hugged and said our goodbyes. While I was waiting for my second bus, guess who showed up? (The enemy) *Yeah, but the 'doctor' said the cancer 'could be' hidden under the lymph nodes."*

STAINED by HIS BLOOD

You know, if you allow the devil to, he would use EVERY negative word that he could to torment you. But before I could even blink, the Holy Spirit quickly stepped in and brought something to my remembrance that I had totally forgotten. He asked me, *"What did the Father have you to do in the beginning, the night before the morning you went in to take your first set of tests?"* I thought about it.... "Oh, He had me to anoint my body with olive oil and told me that I would not have to do this again." I even remember taking a spoonful by mouth. "You see, God does not play tricks or games. He is neither a trickster nor a deceiver but the devil is. Cancer cannot show up and say, 'peek-a-boo'. The medical tests missed me, I hid—Through Jesus Christ **my faith killed it!** With The Holy Spirit Guiding Me Every Step Of The Way! THANK YOU LORD FOR THE HOLY SPIRIT!

STAINED by HIS BLOOD

I thought about it and realized something very, very profound. There is NO PLACE in the Word of God where Jesus half-healed someone. When God heals, He heals COMPLETELY! I rejoiced and praised God as tears rolled down my face and from that day forward, I began telling everyone on the bus and everywhere the Holy Spirit gave me the opportunity to share our testimony that God is still a healer whether one believe it or not. God healed me of ovarian cancer. To God Be The Glory!

STAINED by HIS BLOOD

The next day after putting Ebonee down for her nap, I sat in my living room where it was peaceful. I started talking to God. *"Jesus all those people (in the bible) got a chance to literally walk with you, the woman with the issue of blood, I don't know her name but I really like her. She got a chance to touch the hem of your garment.*

Matthew 9:20,21 says, and behold, a woman, which was diseased with an issue of blood twelve years came behind him, and touched the hem of his garment: For she said within herself, If I may but touch his garment, I shall be whole.

I know this is something she has never forgotten, and I know you know her. I wish I could have done that, I mean just to be able to touch your hem. Father I know that you are within me but, sometimes like now, I really want you here in the mist I want you to hold me, I want you, I lone for your presence right now".

STAINED by HIS BLOOD

Jesus spoke back to me, *"You did touch my garment when you used your faith to be healed, you are closer to me than the ones who walked with me and Mareen I know you. You touched me and we held hands all during your faith fight for your healing and there were times I held you and rocked you to sleep, remember? I am sitting here right next to you.*

I begin turning slowly to my side and could feel Him and I felt His presence like never before, He was there! He was there! Sitting right next to me, He was so close to me. I laid my head in His lap and cried with an uncontrollable joy. He then put His hands on me and he stayed there with me until I was satisfied in my spirit and ready to continue with my daily task for the day.

STAINED by HIS BLOOD

NOTES

CHAPTER 16

7 Steps While Waiting For Your Healing To Manifest

STAINED by HIS BLOOD

STEP ONE<u>: Decide, Decide , if you are going to trust God until your healing is manifested or trust Him to bring you through your surgery.</u>

Ok you have been given an evil report (ungodly words). This report might even shock you or put you at a standstill. Only allow it if you must for a moment, snap out of it. Make a sound decision that you are going to stand in faith no matter how long it is going to take for your healing to manifest. Make up in your mind that no matter what, you are going to believe what **1Peter 2:24** says about you, **Who his own self bare our sins in his own body on the tree, that we, being dead to sins, should live unto righteousness: by whose stripes ye were healed.** Go back and read it. Please make this decision quickly and then trust the Holy Spirit for his guidance.

STAINED by HIS BLOOD

Do not be double minded. A double minded man is unstable in all his ways **James 1:8 in The amplified version says [For being as he is] a man of two minds (hesitating, dubious, irresolute), [he is] unstable and unreliable *and* uncertain about everything [he thinks, feels, decides].**

The decision you make is so key, what you see and hear is very important. When I say decide, it means decide to fight a good fight of faith! To fight a good fight means, to protect your ears in what you hear and listen to. Protect your eyes in what you look at and see. Look at things that are going to edify or build your faith. See yourself healed. I like stories so, here is one:

Robert and I were asked to come out and minister to a friend's daughter who was diagnosed with cancer. When we arrived, she was sitting in the living room watching television. We greeted the family and the daughter as she continued to watch television.

STAINED by HIS BLOOD

Now I don't have a problem with a person watching television but I do when you are watching something that is not helping you, your spirit man needs to grow in faith especially, at a time when you are fighting for your life. The devil is trying to kill you 24/7 if I may put it this way, and you are watching a program called flavor flav (I'm not going to even capitalize the name!) and I might not be saying his name right (who cares). Really! Now, whatever you watch or look at in the privacy of your home is your own business. We did not come to condemn nor judge them. They knew we were coming and even upon entering the home, they did not even attempt to turn it off. I am somewhat glad that they didn't, we then discovered a door the enemy was entering through. I said a door not the door, only a door.

STAINED by HIS BLOOD

There may be other doors but we see this one for sure. One might say Minister Oliver how do you know about that show, well I have children and we have Cable TV in our home. I always go through the channels and lock what we do not want watched throughout our house; not only for our children but also for ourselves you know the flesh love programs like that. If I missed a channel, I believe somehow, The Holy Spirit would show me.

We asked them to turn it off while we were visiting, we believe in ministering to the whole family I mean the ones who live in the same household with the one being challenged. We did not stay long we did what we came to do, gave the word and some advice on some things that needed to be done throughout her healing process. Have you ever been somewhere, where people nodded yes at everything you said, but you felt it was not taken seriously. I think we have all been guilty of thinking we know.

STAINED by HIS BLOOD

Some of us do realize it and change through hearing, teaching and studying the Word of God. This is when one realizes that something is not working for them. They begin to listen and want to know what you did to get a positive result. Sometimes if we do not, have full control of our flesh, it dominates and we do not want to let go of the very thing that is hurting us or preventing us from coming into the full manifestation of our healing or blessing.

I Say You Can!   By studying The Word of God. Ask God to help you and He will send the right people or tools to you, just be ready to receive and know still, that your flesh is going to fight against it. It does not want to let you go or should I say the devil can't stand losing a fight. <u>God Loves You</u> and just like you need Him and you probably don't know it yet He Wants and Need You.

It is so good to be wanted and needed, all at the same time. He has a plan and purpose for your life, find out what it is. He is a God of Love and He likes to show it in many ways. He wants you, to want to spend time with Him, and want you, to want Him to spend time with you. Why would you not want to know what His plan is for your life, and right now it certainly is not death. He loved you before the foundation of this world. Seek Him.

Note: **If you are taking medication or treatments for whatever you have being diagnosed with. Continue to do so, unless instructed by your physician, or The Holy Spirit. Please do not stop, continue to take it as usual and do not feel guilty. The author is not a physician she is just sharing her testimony and The Word of God with you.**

STAINED by HIS BLOOD

STEP TWO: Do not receive or say what you do not want (I am not saying ignore it just do not receive it in your spirit).

Before you can have faith for your healing you must get rid of all negativity and doubt concerning God's will in the matter. God's children must know what the Word of God says about healing. They must know that it is God's will to heal their body; their mind must be renewed to this. Romans 12:2 says, **And be not conformed to this world: but be ye transformed by the renewing of your mind, that ye may prove what is that good, and acceptable, and perfect, will of God.** They must plant the seed, which is the Word of God. Since we are talking about healing, they must plant the seed of healing. When this seed is planted daily faithfully, faith will come and healing will take its place. If you do not plant the seed of healing you won't get a healing harvest. Planting is reading and hearing and doing His Word only. Study it day and night.

STAINED by HIS BLOOD

Get as much information about your diagnosis that comes to your mind if you need to. I am not saying that you need all the facts and the name of it, all the time.

Have something ever bothered you, I mean, have you ever felt a pain in an area of your body and you were not prompted, by The Holy Spirit to go to the doctor to get it checked out. You would just say the Word of God "By Jesus stripes I am healed". Jesus walked around, and healed all sickness and diseases. He healed them all. *Matthew 12:15 But when Jesus knew it, he withdrew himself from thence: and great multitudes followed him, and he healed them all,* You did not even know what it was, you did not even know the name of it but you spoke God's Word and it left. God knows where you are in your faith so allow him to guide you.

STAINED by HIS BLOOD

God works through surgery too, if this is where you are. You still must have faith that God is going to bring you through the surgery and that he will guide that surgeon's hand to perform the surgery.

Whatever decision you make, I suggest that you feed and fill up on the Word of God, especially the four Gospels (Matthew, Mark, Luke and John) during this period in your life. In doing this you will begin a journey with Jesus as he goes from city to city, healing, and delivering people from all manner of sicknesses and diseases.

This will help take your mind off fear. It will renew your mind and strengthen your faith.

You will begin to walk with Jesus as if you were actually with him. You are going to be so excited, because you are actually there spiritually.

STAINED by HIS BLOOD

Really! I cannot explain how the Word comes to reality but it does. Well, yes I can. It is real. The word is alive and as you feed upon it, you will know how alive and true it is, it is not just pages coming from a book it is real and alive. God allows us to travel with Jesus in the Gospels if we really want to.

God cares so, much about us as well, as our circumstances, and the decisions that we make, however, he allows us to make them and He does not push himself on us. He allows you to get close to him as much as you want..... we are his children, that is why as Christian parents we love our kids, and keep them close because we are like our father God. This is so good. You are really in his presence during his walk here on earth. It would be like you are in that time with him.

You become like a disciple in the crowd following him, watching his every move and wanting to be more like him.

STAINED by HIS BLOOD

This means you say what he says, and you love the way he love (unconditional) because your love is going to bring your faith into action. Not worrying! Wow! It is going to be an experience you will never forget. You will be there when they crucify him and you may even shed those tears with his mother Mary. You will share the joy of Mary Magdalene when she found out he had risen. This would build your faith even stronger.

You will know for sure, without a doubt that healing is yours and you will not receive anything else nor will you be moved, by any more-evil reports that are presented to you.

Yes! The devil will try even harder at this point to make you doubt or bring fear of what might be happening to you or in your body. You just have to stand boldly on the Word of God and you will.

STAINED by HIS BLOOD

If for some reason, you are not strong as you should be, then keep reading and studying the word day and night.

Start reading the four gospels over again until you become so full of the word the devil hates it when you get up and you will see then that the evil report will start changing and saying what God's report says about you.

Do not listen to unbelief from any one, as Dr. Dollar says "You are the healed protecting your health, you are not the sick trying to get better". Jesus took care of all of that on the cross. By Jesus stripes, you are healed.

You must see yourself healed, walking, talking, and sharing your beautiful testimony.

STAINED by HIS BLOOD

If the Holy Spirit leads you to have surgery then, someone will want to know that God brought you through your surgery. The devil does not want your healing to manifest or for you to come through that surgery. He wants the praises and he knows that you as a child of the King will tell it. The devil does not want it to spread that our God still heals.

STEP THREE: Do give God all the praise now and worship Him throughout this battle.

Do not wait until you see change on paper, see the change now and praise him for it. Pray, ask God to open your eyes so that you can see yourself healed.

Elisha prayed for his servant in **2Kings 6:17 and Elisha prayed, and said, Lord I pray thee open his eyes, that he may see.** And guess what? The Lord did, **And the Lord opened the spiritual eyes of the young man; and he saw.**

Keep praising him and reading The Word of God for your healing and soon you will see what Jesus seen on the cross. He seen you healed. The devil does not know what to think when you praise God after hearing an evil report or seeing you in pain.

STAINED by HIS BLOOD

If you have a CD player, put your Healing CDs on the repeat button during the night. Sleep with The Word on every night. This seems to be the time that is most challenging. This is the time you might feel the most pain, be in doubt and fear. But don't you be afraid stay in Faith you are not alone Christ lives Big within you and you have angels that are encamped all around you so please don't say anything contrary to what the word says about you. Say words such as, 1Peter 2:24"**By His Stripes (I Am) Healed" and** 1John 4:4b**"Greater Is He That Is In You, Than He That Is In The World"**.

Psalms 34:7 says, **The Angel of the Lord encamps around those who fear Him [who revere and worship Him with awe] and each of them He delivers.** (Amplified)

Deuteronomy 31:6 says, **Be strong and of good courage, fear not, nor be afraid of them: For the Lord thy God, he it is that doth go with thee; he will not fail thee nor forsake thee. Only say what The Word of God says and you will be alright.**

STAINED by HIS BLOOD

STEP FOUR: **You need to know that your family and friends love you and want to give you advice. Stay in love.** You must only hear and obey the Word of God. The Holy Spirit will tell you or confirm it in your spirit if he sends a word to you through someone. At this point in your life you are in a war, a faith war, and not only here on earth, but you are fighting in the spirit realm for your life, so you have to be careful of the company and atmosphere you are surrounded by. There may be people that want to touch you, or lay hands on you, that maybe ok, and then again, it may not be. Listen for the Holy Spirit, Wait for Him to give an ok. His presence have to be there, if you are not sure then don't you allow it. You will be all right trust God. You will not miss out on anything when you have the Word of God. It might sound right but it might not be right for that person to pray or lay hands on you.

STAINED by HIS BLOOD

This is very important. You do not want everyone to know that you are fighting in a faith war, although they mean well, and they do, their faith may not be where it needs to be to help you fight this war, or even stand in faith with you. Just say thank you or no thank you in the kindness way you know how. The enemy wants your faith, He hates your faith when it is use to bring God's Word to pass, even when you are standing in faith for someone else. The enemy will try everything to make you doubt God's Word. You stand on your faith. Your faith is will bring your healing to manifestation, along with your love walk, do everything in love, **No Strife,** Strife will hinder or kill your faith. This will be the number one way I believe the enemy will come at you; this could wipe out your faith if you allow **Strife** in. You don't have time for this, You are in battle and you win if you faint not, Strife is a spirit that the enemy uses against God's children to destroy them if they allow it.

STAINED by HIS BLOOD

Faith is a spirit, which can be used against the devil; it kills the spirit of doubt and pleases God. If a person insist on praying for you just tell them to pray for your strength. Let us talk a little about love. You must continue to love, this is a very sensitive time for you, you should do this anyway I mean walk in love always. Do it on purpose, even though it can be a challenge at times. Remember, this is a way the enemy can come in, and steal what belongs to you, your healing and your peace etc. Please be quick to forgive others, unforgiveness is another spirit that can stand in your way of receiving your healing. Do not let your shield of faith down.

Stay in faith even if you do not feel like it. Faith is not a feeling. Faith is knowing that you are healed, no matter how you feel. If you get to a point where you are feeling physically tired, then it could be that you are fighting in the flesh. Keep your spiritual body up. Read the word day and night.

STAINED by HIS BLOOD

Overdose on it. Keep your spiritual body strong your physical body will catch up to it.

The war that you are in is not a fleshy fight, it is a faith fight, you can fight this fight successfully in the spirit realm, and you can only do this through The Word of God. Ephesians 6: 12 says, For we wrestle not against principalities, against powers, against the rulers of the darkness of this world, against spiritual wickedness in high places.

If you are feeling weak in your physical body do not announce it, do not say I am weak or I am getting weaker every day. Putting those words out in the atmosphere only gives satan the power to inflict more pain on you. You are a Warrior say what Joel 3:10b says, **Let the weak say, I am strong.**

Keep your mind on The Word… Everything else is secondary.

STEP FIVE: <u>Only have people that God has appointed for you to have around you, and for you to be around.</u>

If you are not sure about someone, then I advise you to pray. Pray in the Holy Ghost (tongues). You should be doing this a lot and this is so the devil will not know what you are sharing with your father God. It is between you and God. This is so special. The devil will be so confused on what to say to you through people and what to do. This is when he just starts throwing things at you. You just keep throwing the word back at him because about this time, it will be all you know to say. You will be full of the word. If you don't know what decision to make, whether it's surgery, chemotherapy or to stand in faith using no assistance from outside of The Word of God, just pray about it, God will give you an answer and you will have a peace about it(smile).

STAINED by HIS BLOOD

STEP SIX: **Every negative thought or pain you feel in your natural body must be fought with the Word.**

Use scriptures to defend yourself. You do not need a whole list of scriptures to memorize to do this, just one, two, maybe three. However, as you keep reading and studying the Word of God, more scriptures will come to mind (I have listed some healing scriptures for you on the last page of this book). The Holy Ghost will help you to remember them and all that you need to know at this time. If you keep fighting with the word, you will see the physical body yielding to the spiritual body. It will obey every word of God you say out of your mouth and you will find yourself getting stronger each day. Let me share this with you (a story).

STAINED by HIS BLOOD

In 2004, my husband and I ran the Chicago Marathon and I would not have finished it if I had not known the Word of God. I was in so much pain, I knew that quitting was not an option for me but I needed to know how I was going to finish this race. God put this race on our hearts to do and complete because it was more than about running a marathon. Anyway, somewhere between miles 19 or 21, I had leg cramps in both of my legs, so I was moving slowly. I remember the word that we were taught during the first month of training with the Elijah Running Club at our church. I had to ignore my burning feet and thighs. I had to pull this strength from above. I quoted scriptures and spoke in tongue all the rest of the way to the finish line, 26.2 miles. What I am saying is that the physical body will try to give up, but the spiritual body, if it has been fed with the right kind of food, which is The Word of God, it will overpower and take over the flesh because we are spirits first.

With every breath, you take say the word only such as "By Jesus stripes I am healed", "Jesus is Lord", "I shall live and not die and declare the works of the Lord".

You will become just like Jesus. You will speak the word only. Scriptures will flow out of your mouth so easily because you have studied the word day and night. You have become one with the word of God. Your strength, your joy, your faith will become so strong that this fight will become so easy to you because now you know who you are and what belongs to you. "Healing is yours and it's your choice to either live here on earth longer or go home to be with our father, it's all up to you.

I totally agree with Pastor Daryl Barnett he says, **"Either way you win However, what a Testimony if you stay!"**

STEP SEVEN: <u>**Now that your report has lined up with The Word of God, do not let your guard down continue to read and study The Word of God and praying always (in your spiritual tongues) and praising God for your healing.**</u>

Do not get relaxed just keep inhaling The Word of God, this should be or become a way of life for you. Keep inhaling (reading and hearing) The Word and The Word is what you will exhale. The enemy is always waiting for an opportunity to come in, just to see if you are still what you say you are (healed). A pain might come; a negative report might even be presented to you again. You need to say "Devil You Are a Liar by His Stripes I Am Still Healed". You are not in remission you are healed.

STAINED by HIS BLOOD

Remission means you are pardoned and you are forgiven. There is not a statement made or written anywhere in His Word saying He healed them and now they are in remission. <u>"I do not think so Saints"</u>.

The word remission is used in **Mark1:4 "John did baptize in the wilderness, and preach the baptism of repentance for the remission of sins"**.

Acts 2:38 says, Then Peter said unto them, Repent and be baptized every one of you in the name of Jesus Christ for the remission of sins, and ye shall receive the gift of the Holy Ghost.

Hebrews 10:18 says, Now where remission of these is, there is no more offering for sin.

Let us not use the word remission when God has healed us, you are healed or, you are not healed, but you are not in remission.

STAINED by HIS BLOOD

Using the word remission means, you are in doubt about your healing you are waiting for death to come in and take you. You are waiting for illness to return any day or time now.

This is what you are saying when you say I am in remission or when you receive this word from a physician.

I remember an incident some years ago I went with Robert to an event where he was modeling. I sat at a table with a woman who told me she use to have cancer. I thought wow we could share testimonies about how God healed us. Her testimony started out sounding very good, I recognized our father God in it until she said she was in remission. I asked her did she believe and received healing through Jesus Christ, because there is no remission in healing in Him. Either you are healed or you are not. She replied again that she was in remission and that she knows it is going to come back.

STAINED by HIS BLOOD

She totally dismissed what I was telling her. I said it is not coming back; I was trying to speak a positive word in her life. I told her to trust God; continue to read His Word and receive your healing and your faith will grow to where you will not believe that the cancer will come back.

She went on and said Yes! It is going to come back, and I know it (hum, I thought). This conversation went on for a while with me trying to convince her about healing.

The event was beginning to start, doors were being closed and the lights became dimmed. She started to talk even more, this time she brought up another problem she was dealing with besides being in remission. She said she had claustrophobia this came up when they closed the doors.

She kept looking back at the doors and saying she cannot stay in a close room to long, the event was about an hour and half.

STAINED by HIS BLOOD

In my mind at this time I was thinking "Who invited her and whose guess is she. Is she going to talk through the whole event, My God! We were not too far from the doors so, if she felt she needed to go out she could. Did she think this event was going to be outside? She kept talking, talking, and mumbling about being in remission and the doors.

About this time, I was tired of hearing her unbelief and I was not going to convince her anymore about being healed. I wanted her to go and go now! I was feeling a little exhausted I felt like I had been in a fight a physical fight.

Hey, Child of God, Do not let people do this to you, just walk away politely or change your seat and do not forget to pray for them. *"Tell them you want to get a seat closer and make sure that it is only one seat available"* unfortunately; there was not another seat in the place, I could move to. I allowed her to talk to me one last time. She said the same thing she was saying before the event and during the event.

STAINED by HIS BLOOD

I said to her nicely, *Yes! honey, the cancer will come back, you are inviting it to come back with open arms.*

I am praying that you do not speak those negative words and maybe you should leave now because I do not want you to feel sick while waking out the doors. Her respond was Yes!, I had better leave now because they closed the doors. *Ok I said, and have a good day I will be praying for you* .The devil had her blind and deceived so, that she would not even hear The Word of God.

STAINED by HIS BLOOD

Now that your report has lined up with God's report, Continue to keep His Word before you. There is so much of God to know and learn about and being His child, there is so much He wants us to know about Him. This will be the exciting part, getting to know more about Him. We get to know more about Him as we continue to study, read and hear about other people who have experienced being in his presence.

One more thing; look into changing your diet if you need to. Eating the wrong foods could delay the manifestation of your healing and could open a door for sickness and disease. Dr. Veronica Winston has a book on this called "Health and Nutrition" and she has a 30-day devotional called "Devine Health". I am sure there are many several books along with these but these are the ones I have read.

A nutrient class may help or a special diet from your physician. Include some light exercise routines <u>if permitted</u> make sure you check with your physician. Some of us have jobs, children, and a spouse to tend to daily. This will keep our minds occupied when we are not in The Word.

STAINED by HIS BLOOD

WHO I AM IN CHRIST (CONFESSION)

Father God I thank you that I am like a tree that is planted by the rivers of water and I will not be moved. I bear fruit in its season without fail and everything I do according to your Word will prosper, Father I declare I am your child and joint heir with Christ; therefore you have given me all things. I thank you that in all situations that I face I am more than a conqueror through Christ who loves me. And for my sake Father God you made Christ to be sin for me who knew no sin, so that in and through Him I might become the righteousness of You, I proclaim it is you who have made me what I am and you have given me a new life recreated in Christ that I may do your will which you have predestined for me to walk in, Therefore I will be strong, in you Father God and in the power of your might and draw all my strength and power from you through your Word. I profess that I am complete in you, who is the head of all principalities and power and I pronounce that satan have not one ounce of power over me, he cannot cause me to be fearful, or cause me to worry nor ever think that my God has forsaken me. Knowing this, I receive great and precious promises that you Father God have given me that through these promises, I am a partaker of your divine nature and will not sin against you. In Jesus Name, Amen.

STAINED by HIS BLOOD

Prayer of Salvation

Father God I come to you in the Name of Your Son, Jesus Christ. You said in Your Word that whosoever shall call upon the Name of the Lord shall be saved, according to Romans 10:13. I believe Jesus came and died on the cross for my sins and that He was raised from the dead on the third day with all power in His hands. Lord Jesus I am asking You to come into my heart. I receive You as my Lord and Savior over my life right now in Jesus 'Name Amen.

Welcome to the family of Our Lord and Savior.

If you do not have a church home ask God to help you find one, A Word Church that teaches **The Full Gospel** from Genesis to Revelation this include Baptism of The Holy Spirit (speaking in tongues).

Make sure you get water baptize immediately after The Prayer of Salvation.

Baptism comes from the Greek word "baptizo" which means to dip, to immerse or to submerge; So therefore baptism done in any other way is not Biblical; it is not a baptism at all(Strong's Concordance)

Water Baptism is so important, in the book of Acts when one would teach about Jesus Christ the people responded by being baptized in the water according to **Acts 16:31-33**. You may want to read the whole Chapter of Acts 16 to get a better picture or understanding or just read the whole book, it is all good.

Paul taught that water baptism was our way of identifying with the death of Jesus Christ, this is found in, **Romans 6:4 and Colossians 2:12.**

STAINED by HIS BLOOD

My favorite scripture is **Galatians 2:20, I am crucified with Christ: nevertheless I live; yet not I , but Christ liveth in me: and the life which I now live in the flesh I live by the faith of the Son of God, who loved me, and gave himself for me.**

The Amplified Bible puts it this way, **I have been crucified with Christ [in Him I have shared His crucifixion]; it is no longer I who live, but Christ (the Messiah) lives in me; and the life I now live in the body I live by faith in(by adherence to and reliance on and complete trust in) the Son of God, Who loved me and gave Himself up for me.**

Adherence - steady or faithful attachment.
Reliance – something or someone relied on.

STAINED by HIS BLOOD

Prayer For Baptism Of The Holy Spirit

My Heavenly Father, I am Your child, for I believe in my heart that Jesus has been raised from the dead and I have confessed Him as my Lord.

Jesus said, "How much more shall your heavenly Father give the Holy Spirit to those who ask Him." I ask You now in the Name of Jesus to fill me with the Holy Spirit. I step into the fullness and power that I desire in the Name of Jesus. I confess that I am a Spirit-filled Christian. As I yield my vocal organs, I expect to speak in tongues for the Spirit gives me utterance in the Name of Jesus. Praise the Lord! Amen.

Scriptures References:

John 14:16-17	Acts 10:44-46
Luke 11:13	Acts 19: 2, 5-6
Acts 1:8a	1 Corinthians 14:2-15
Acts 2:4	1 Corinthians 14:18, 27
Acts 2:32, 33, 39	Ephesians 6:18
Acts 8:12-17	Jude 1:20

STAINED by HIS BLOOD

Healing Medicine

Exodus 15:26, 23:25

Deuteronomy 7:15, 28:1-14, 61, 30:19, 20

1Kings 8:56

Psalm 91:16, 103:3, 107:20, 118:17

Proverbs 4:20-23

Isaiah 41:10, 53:4, 5

Jeremiah 1:12, 30:17

Joel 3:10

Nahum 1:9

Matthew 8:2, 3, 8:17, 18:18, 19, 21:21

Mark 11:23, 24, 16:17, 18

John 10: 10

STAINED by HIS BLOOD

Romans 4:17-20, 8:11

2Corinthians 10:4, 5

Galatians 3:13, 14

Ephesians 6:10-17

Philippians 4:6, 7

2Timothy 1:7

Hebrews 10:23, 35, 11:11, 13:8

James 5:14, 15

1Peter 2:24

1John 3:21, 22

3John 2

Revelations 12:11

STAINED by HIS BLOOD

Dedication

To all of my siblings: James, Linda, Sheree, Michael, Algeria, Anita, Sharon and Moe.

To my other sisters and brothers, I love you so much: Latonya Briggs, Robert Parker(Cecil), Margea Chenault, Elaine Parker, Donald & Macie Robinson, Sharon Seanor, Angela Brassfield, Ceil Sykes,

Francine Taylor, Patrice Baker, Nicholle Winston, Torshia Frank, and Phyllis Flynn.

To all my family and friends, I pray that this book blesses you and encourages you to continue to get to know God more and have a deeper relationship with him. I encourage you to continue to allow Him to be first in your life and to let His word be the final authority in your life.

STAINED by HIS BLOOD

In memory of

Some special people that have passed through my life and whom I hold dear in my heart:

My sister and brother: Marsha Peoples and Lamont Williams.

My grandmothers Sadie Mae Bland (big momma) and Lillie McKinney.

My daddy, James Oliver Sr. (father-in law).

My great aunt, Daisy Gordon.

My aunt and uncles Irene Smith, Homer Smith and Jimmy Peoples.

My godmother, Barbara McClinton.

My godson, Jesse L. Brown Jr.

My nephew, Schunklin Williams.

My brother in law, Marc. A. Oliver

My cousins, Sharon Gordon, Deborah Gordon, and Sonya Shears.

<u>My family in Christ</u>

Asia Carr, Linda Young, Mary Williams, Linda Lucas Kristen Squire, and Calvin Rhyne.

STAINED by HIS BLOOD

ABOUT THE AUTHOR

Mareen Oliver along with her husband is a member of Living Word Christian Center in Forest Park, Illinois under the leadership of Dr. William S. Winston.

Mareen and her husband are founders of "Sleeping With The Word Outreach Ministries. She is a graduate of Living Word Christian Center School of Ministry.

Mareen has been married to her husband, Robert G. Oliver Sr. for 25years, they have four children: Robert Jr., Ebonee, Brandy and Tanisha.

STAINED by HIS BLOOD

Mission Statement

To teach the true Word of God and empower others through the love of Jesus Christ with the guidance of the Holy Spirit.

Vision Statement

To fulfill God's purpose in my life and to help others fulfill God's purpose in their lives and to lead the unsaved to our Lord and Savior Jesus Christ.

STAINED by HIS BLOOD

Books by Mareen Oliver

Who's Behind It?

Stained By His Blood: The Promise